PENGUIN BOOKS
WAR STORIES

Gaylene Preston is a film producer and director. Her extensive catalogue of independently made films grew out of her work as an art therapist in the United Kingdom, where she made her first film as part of a drama therapy project with institutionalised patients at Fulbourn Hospital, Cambridge. Twenty years later she is one of New Zealand's best known film makers. Her feature films include *Mr Wrong, Ruby and Rata* and *Bread and Roses*. Gaylene Preston's films have won awards in Australia, Canada, France, Italy and Switzerland. In her latest film, *War Stories*, Gaylene Preston has combined the two film-making forms she most enjoys: the reality and immediacy of documentary with the scope, drama and narrative structure of the feature film. *War Stories*, the film, was made in conjunction with this book.

Judith Fyfe has worked as a broadcaster in radio and television in New Zealand for over twenty-five years. She is also an experienced scriptwriter for television drama, and is the author of *Matriarchs* (1990) and, with Hugo Manson, *The Gamble—The Campaign Diary of the Challengers: Snap Election 1984*. Co-founder and former executive director of the New Zealand Oral History Archive, Judith Fyfe is one of the country's leading oral historians. She was awarded a Fulbright Scholarship in 1987 to carry out research into and lecture on oral history in the United States. She is working on a series of contemporary as well as historical projects. Judith Fyfe is currently studying law at Victoria University and lives in Wellington.

For the children

OUR MOTHERS NEVER TOLD US

PENGUIN BOOKS

PENGUIN BOOKS

Penguin Books (NZ) Ltd, 182–190 Wairau Road, Auckland 10, New Zealand
Penguin Books Ltd, 27 Wrights Lane, London W8 5TZ, England
Penguin USA, 375 Hudson Street, New York, NY 10014, United States
Penguin Books Australia Ltd, 487 Maroondah Highway, Ringwood, Australia 3134
Penguin Books Canada Ltd, 10 Alcorn Avenue, Toronto, Ontario, Canada M4V 3B2

Penguin Books Ltd, Registered Offices: Harmondsworth, Middlesex, England

First published in 1995
1 2 3 4 5 6 7 8 9 10
Copyright © Gaylene Preston Productions 1995

All rights reserved. Without limiting the rights under copyright reserved above, no part of this publication may be reproduced, stored in or introduced into a retrieval system, or transmitted, in any form or by any means (electronic, mechanical, photocopying, recording or otherwise), without the prior written permission of both the copyright owner and the above publisher of this book.

Editorial services by Michael Gifkins and Associates
Designed by Reidy Design and Associates
Printed in New Zealand

CONTENTS

Preface 7

Introduction 9

Pamela Quill 19

Doreen Foss 35

Tui Preston 46

Jean Andrews 71

Flo Small 92

Ali Doyle 115

Mabel Waititi 129

Rita Graham 143

Neva Clarke McKenna 162

Appendix I: 186
Chronology of women's work 1940-1946

Appendix II: 188
The Women in War *oral history project*

Acknowledgements

My thanks go
to my brother, Edward, and sister, Jan, for their support; Robin Laing, who raised some money where my mouth was; to Ray Grover, who gave the first wholehearted support from a major institution; to Sharon Dell, who provided early support without needing many pieces of paper; to Sue Thompson, who cared far more than she needed to; and most of all to Judith Fyfe, without whom this project wouldn't have had a donkey's chance. Thanks for your thorough attention to detail, your intelligence, eloquence and understanding, and, most of all, your great good humour.
Gaylene Preston

Our thanks, also, to everyone who has participated in or contributed in some way to the different stages—from oral history project to book and film—in particular: Sharon Dell, assistant chief librarian, Hugo Manson and Jim Sullivan, managers, Oral History Centre, Joan McCracken, librarian, Pictorial Reference Service, and other staff of the Alexander Turnbull Library; Jock Phillips, Chief Historian, Historical Branch, Department of Internal Affairs; Clive Sowry at National Archives; Carey Johnson and Sarah Dalton, OH project managers; Jane Tolerton, Alison Parr, Brita McVeigh, Jillian Riddle, project contributors; Cerridwyn Young, Editorial Production Assistant; Susan Fowke and Queenie Rikihana-Hyland, principal researchers/interviewers; all the interviewers, and of course the interviewees.

Thanks also to Lauris Edmond, Carolyn Milward, Nancy Taylor and others who have collected and published stories and information relating to New Zealand women and the Second World War.

The New Zealand People at War: Home Front, the official history of New Zealand in the Second World War by Nancy M. Taylor, and *Brief Encounter: American Forces and the New Zealand People 1942–1945* by Jock Phillips with Ellen Ellis, both published by the Historical Publications Branch of Internal Affairs, 1986 and 1992, have been valuable resources for the preparation of the introductory material to the book.

We acknowledge the Alexander Turnbull Library, National Library of New Zealand, for permission to reproduce their archival photographs on the cover and within the book. Acknowledgement is also made to Gaylene Preston for the contemporary photographs of the interviewees, and to the private collections whose photographs are reproduced. The lyrics of 'As Time Goes By' (Hupfield/Warner) are reprinted with permission of J. Albert & Son Propriety Ltd, with all rights reserved.
Gaylene Preston, *Judith Fyfe*

Preface

War Stories. I don't know how I started collecting them. I suppose I grew up in the shadow of the war. During the peace. Back then, to me as a small child, there were three times: 'before-the-war', 'after-the-war' and, the most secret time of all, 'during-the-war'.

I heard stories around my mother's skirts. Sitting under the kitchen table while the women talked above me. Never about the battles or the bombs. Always about the relationships, dislocated and wrenched apart or, sometimes worse, forced together again because of that time called 'during-the-war'.

The men's stories were very different. Not only in context, but in the telling. They were recounted loudly with a beer in one hand, a rollie in the other and eruptions of laughter. Army yarns for public consumption. Sometimes the voices would become serious and a small silence would fill the room, but not for long. The show must go on Lest We Forget.

Everyone was trying to, I realise now. Desperately seeking that amnesia that blocks out thoughts of waste and futility and turns them into mythology. Because we won. It had to have been worth it. So my whole generation grew up in the bright piercing light of the peacetime. The fifties. Security. Conformity and everyone living the same happily-ever-after, with the deep shadow of the war largely unacknowledged.

I suppose it's hard to own a war as a first-hand event when it didn't happen here. When you live in a little piece of pink on the edge of the British Empire in a place where hardly a shot was fired. No apocalypse here. No blitz. No death and carnage. Just romantic photos on the mantelpiece of young soldiers who never came back. Who never had funerals and who stayed forever young encased in the black and white reality of an Egyptian photographer's studio portrait. And those who did come back, often could only confront the terror in their worst nightmares. Sissy stuff. No demobbing. No therapy. No 'let's talk it over'. Just roll your sleeves up and work it off.

But down among the women the war was an on-going event. It was the reason why a neighbour never married, or couldn't have babies, or another's husband drank. Why a father rejected a son, why a husband couldn't be loving.

I used to think they were a timid bunch, these women, with their naïve unworldly ways and their insistence on conformity and security, but I now know how wrong I was.

Reluctantly at first, because they all felt their stories weren't important, they have with great candour and frankness, told us tales that vividly evoke their lives and times. The nine stories in this book haven't been found after years of careful searching. Carefully selected they are, and it has taken a few years, but 57 similar stories are now lodged on sound tape in the Alexander Turnbull Library, and there's plenty more where they came from. Ask your grandmothers.

I have found the experience of knowing these women and listening to their stories a very humbling and inspiring one. Humbling because I suppose in my supreme confidence, I thought my generation invented everything; and inspiring because of who these women are. Their humility and deep understanding is a testament to the overwhelming triumph of the human spirit.

Unsurprisingly, I suppose, one of them is my mother. I would like to thank her and the other women in this book for coming clean and telling it like it was.

You must remember this
A kiss is still a kiss
A sigh is just a sigh
The fundamental things apply
As time goes by.

Gaylene Preston

Introduction

War Stories is not a book about the war. It is a collection of stories about an event that was universal—the Second World War—and how it was experienced and remembered very differently by individual New Zealand women, young women who found themselves in strange circumstances that were beyond their control.

This is a collection of stories that have never been written before, and have only now been spoken. Because they were too personal, too painful, too inappropriate, or too revealing—these are the stories that our mothers never told us.

Fifty years ago New Zealand families gathered around their radios in the evening of Sunday 3 September to hear the voice of a man, literally thousands of miles away on the other side of the world, declare that Britain was at war with Germany. This meant New Zealand was at war too because, as Prime Minister Savage proclaimed soon after, 'Where she goes, we go. Where she stands, we stand.' Because this was the era of global radio communication, the announcement had an immediate impact and, before people even had time to think about it, an irreversible shift had occurred.

The first move was made by the men. Within three days, in New Zealand over 25,000 of them volunteered to go to war. By the end of it more than 150,000 had served in the armed forces. While the men focused on the requirements of a war, the women took over the day-to-day running of the country and for the next six years many young women experienced something that their mothers never had—they had jobs and their own income and for a time they were honorary men.

That was half a century ago. In writing today about the Second World War one is aware that most of the details of the war are known and don't require explanation to a particular generation of New Zealanders. But even those who were the participants are only just now starting to make sense of this huge historical event. During the war itself it was impossible to have an objective view of it. Then as time passed and it became history the kaleidoscope of facts and feelings were assembled into a manageable and publicly acceptable version of 'the war'. Memories of the war became collective and stratified.

And that is the packaged account that has been handed down from the war generation to the next. It was a generation that had a remarkable capacity to 'put things out of their mind'. Even if they did think about things, they did not speak about them. This is hardly surprising when you consider that one of the messages repeated very firmly throughout the war was to 'shut up'—to button up and say nothing, because 'loose lips lose lives'. During the war people got used to talking with caution. Even private conversations were guarded, in case 'someone' was listening.

There are other reasons why this generation seems to be strangely silent and secretive. Immediately after the war, the experiences were often too painful or too confusing to talk about. Sometimes the private feelings didn't conform with public opinion or perception about the war and therefore they had to be internalised or repressed.

Once the war was over people wanted to forget the past and get on with the future. When eventually life was some distance from the event and people might have wanted to talk, there was a new barrier—attitudes had changed. The glorification of war was condemned. By the 1970s, the sons and daughters of 'the war generation' were vocally anti-war. Rather than respond to this disapproval of what they had done, their parents largely retreated, keeping their feelings to themselves and leaving that part of their life's story to the official war records and military histories.

Thousands upon thousands of words have been written about the Second World War, but remarkably few of them about the everyday lives of New Zealand women during the war. War has traditionally been viewed as a predominantly male domain. Because women were not on the combat or lethal side of war, their role was in the broadest sense one of nurturing, supporting and supplying. This was regarded as an essential but secondary wartime role and it has not had the glamour or importance ascribed to a frontline position. It has never been described as an equal partnership. But obviously whatever affected the men then correspondingly affected the women, and vice versa. The war, both directly and indirectly, changed or reshaped their lives just as it did the men's. (It is interesting to speculate that if there is a Third World War it is unlikely that New Zealand women will be 'manpowered'. It is more likely that women will take their part in frontline activities alongside men and that the roles may be reversed so that men stay home to raise the children and manage the civilian services.)

'War babies' and 'baby boomers', people like Gaylene Preston and I, have become interested in the generation that raised us and as a result they have started to speak more openly about their wartime experiences. Both of us have a particular interest in the voices of our mothers and aunts, and women like them—we wanted to hear *their* versions of the war.

Little research has been done into the experiences and attitudes of women—about how they themselves perceive that brief period of their lives. Was it the best, the worst time, the least or the most interesting, a liberating or insignificant time of their life? The answers to those

questions have remained a mystery even to the women themselves.

Because we think the impact the war had on our mothers and women like them (and of course subsequently on us) is important, we decided the imbalance needed to be addressed, and we wanted those questions answered. This curiosity led to the commissioning of a major oral history project, 'New Zealand Women In World War Two', carried out between 1991 and 1994 (a report and methodology are at the back of this book). The objective was not to compare men's and women's wartime experiences, but to inquire about a relative period of silence by recording hitherto undocumented oral testimonies. Basically we wanted to know the short- and long-term emotional and psychological affects the war had on them. We were more interested in how they felt about that period in *their* lives, rather than what they actually *did*.

The project resulted in the recording of in-depth interviews with 66 women about their perspective of the war, primarily for archival purposes, but always with the intention that the project would be the resource for other works, in particular the film *War Stories* and this book.

Themes and issues became apparent, and it emerged from the research that there were five main categories of women in their twenties and early thirties, during the war:

Married with young children with husband at home. Settled routine, relatively stable, day-to-day lives. Usually say they 'didn't do anything in the war' but in fact they did an enormous amount of volunteer war and patriotic fundraising work.

Married with children, but husband serving overseas. Also claim that they 'didn't do anything' during the war. Very few were in any form of paid work. Effectively solo parents organising their own lives, managing their own finances and making their own decisions. Often returned to live with their parents, so had an extended family base. Those who didn't were usually in a less satisfactory situation often living in lonely bedsits with virtually no child care available.

Married, with no children, husband overseas. In some ways this is the most complicated category. They were neither 'single' nor were they mothers. They were working in order to support themselves or because they were manpowered. There was something heroic about this group—the 'woman waiting', the bride without a partner.

Single women. Working, unless there was a good reason. Either manpowered out of their existing jobs into essential war or industrial work, or into jobs left vacant when the men went overseas. Some were jobs traditionally done by men but most would be defined as 'women's work'. There was a swelling in the bottom-ranked occupations rather than a storming of the executive or professional offices. The demand increased for women to go to work as the war continued (in 1942 all women aged 18–30 were ordered to register for direction to essential work). Some loved being manpowered, others loathed and resented it. Many involved themselves with patriotic fundraising, the entertainment of troops or concert parties. They often took advantage of the extra social life that started with farewells for the boys and then moved on to 'dance duty' at parties and socials organised for the servicemen and the visiting American marines.

Single and in the services. The auxiliary services to the navy, army and the air force. Predominantly in nursing positions, some clerical and a few in more technical departments, communications and transport. They were in uniform, had rank and either stayed at home or went overseas to the Middle East, Europe or North Africa. About 10,000 New Zealand women of eligible age went into the services. They are like a breed apart, particularly those commissioned overseas. They had position, skills that were recognised and paid for and new experiences. Almost invariably they say that they gained confidence and self-respect. Unlike those that claimed they 'did nothing during the war', servicewomen had a great deal to talk about.

War was a time of heightened emotions. People fell in love very easily; there was an urgency that gave romance an edge and the instability added a certain zest to daily life. Virtual strangers made lifetime commitments. One of the milestones for a number of women in New Zealand was the wartime presence of American men— generally known as 'the American invasion'. In 1942, as 20,000 New Zealand men left the country, 25,000 American men arrived. (A hundred thousand were based here between mid-1942 and mid-1944.)

Many New Zealanders still think that the American troops were based in this country to protect us from the Japanese because the British couldn't, but in reality New Zealand became strategically important when the allies put the South West Pacific theatre into US military care. This country was a convenient and safe base unlikely to be attacked. It was also a food supplier for the American services and a place for sick servicemen to recuperate and for rest and recreation.

New Zealand women were generally impressed with the Americans. Hollywood manifested itself right here, 'down under'. They all looked like Clark Gable (numerous women raved about their 'great teeth'!). Basically the 'Yanks', as they were called with affection or with disparagement, had more money, more manners and more panache than the Kiwi blokes. They taught our girls how to jitterbug, do the swing and enjoy jazz, and they showered them with gifts of chocolates, flowers and highly desired nylon stockings.

Women had fun—they had a good and memorable time with the Yanks, who set new standards of male behaviour which women then wanted their own brothers and boyfriends to emulate. Many Kiwi males did not like being told to 'smarten up' by their girlfriends and wives. On the one hand the men were grateful for the protection they believed the Americans were providing against enemy invasion but on the other they resented the fact that while 'our boys' were away fighting, the Yanks, loaded with money, were off with their women. This may explain the somewhat ambivalent attitude toward Americans in New Zealand, even today.

There are many, many myths about 'the American invasion', but there is no doubt that heads and hearts were turned momentarily and permanently. The year after their arrival there was a bulge in the statistics. The birth rate of children born out of wedlock rose significantly. There was an almost parallel rise in the rate of deaths of women from septicaemia as a result of back street or illegal abortions. These deaths should probably be included in the records as 'death due to war'. In March 1943, *Truth* newspaper expressed alarm at the number of abortions being carried out and claimed that 30 to 40 abortion cases were admitted each week to Auckland Public Hospital.

The lives of many New Zealand women—the knowing and experienced as well as the innocent—were affected, directly and indirectly, by the Americans who introduced glamour, style and courtesy, and sometimes tragedy, into their lives. Who you slept with during the war is just as relevant as what you *did* in the war. It is a legitimate and seminal question in searching to find out what exactly did happen to the lives of young women during the war. Although this generation largely denies there was sex before marriage, the figures and anecdotal evidence tell us otherwise.

Wartime music and dancing seems to be the motif for these women. Dancing was more than just an excuse to get 'all dolled up'. It was a chance to dream and fantasise; an opportunity to get away from work at home, work at work, the daily drone of family life, and feel beautiful and desirable—to feel something more than your ordinary, everyday self. For young women in the 1940s, who led relatively restricted lives compared to young women these days, it was a freedom and physical pleasure with no strings attached. It stretched the thin line between childhood and marriage.

In many ways the war brought an end to the traditional extended family life. There were too many gaps in family gatherings after the war, and carefree families became remorseful families. Fathers and brothers turned into sour men and mothers were physically and emotionally exhausted by two world wars and a depression. 'Normal life' of pre-war days was out of reach, and for many women the next five years—the post-war period of readjustment—was in some ways even more traumatic than the war itself had been. They had to re-establish their relationships with their partners, get used to having a man as head of the household again and help their children adjust to living with fathers who were or had become virtual strangers.

When the men came back from overseas and took back their jobs, the women left the factories, the streets, the fields and the offices and returned to the kitchen. But it wasn't the same kitchen and it was different from their mothers'. Not only were there new materials and equipment but the home had changed. Even the layout altered as houses were designed to meet the needs of the new nuclear family—part of the rejection of communal living. Everyone wanted a home of their own—away from the in-laws or mum and dad, because they had lived too long together under orders—and because they'd stepped out and dipped their toes into the pleasures of living their own lives.

After the war some were adamant, particularly ex-servicewomen, that it was a job and income that they needed—their priority was a career, not a man. The feminist movement of the seventies did not happen in limbo. Perhaps, as one woman suggested, if unspoken thoughts and ambitions are passed on through the genes, then subconsciously they passed on to their daughters the resentment, never voiced, about the forced reversion to the old roles of wifehood. Maybe they transferred to their daughters their ambitions that women should be equal to men, rather than secondary.

From the study it was not possible to judge to what extent the war shaped the personalities and destinies of these women. The situations they were in were not identical and generally the individual perceptions and responses were different. The times for some, particularly if they were married with children, were not that extraordinary. War, for them, was alongside three meals a day. Life carried on more or less as normal. While the sheer diversity of reaction and response was significant, the one thing they had almost unanimously in common was the opinion that war was a terrible thing. They felt the loss, the futility and the cost were too great. A number expressed disgust at how a few could manipulate the lives of millions.

Despite their anti-war feelings most felt it was an important period in their lives. Some even felt that they had gained more than they lost but in most cases it is only now, in hindsight, that they are able to realise this. But for everyone, the war changed the world; it was not the same afterwards. This book does not deal with that tumultuous time of social upheaval, but these stories

hint at why those dramatic changes occurred.

War Stories is the outcome of the documentary film and the oral history project. From the oral history project a small group of women were selected as representative of the many wartime experiences, but with distinctive ones of their own. Finally nine of them retold parts of their war histories on film in interviews with myself and Gaylene Preston. The stories in this book result from the transcripts of both the filmed and the audio interviews. In the text we have retained the grammar for the ear rather than the eye, so that the individual voices can be heard.

The interview process was for some the equivalent of a confessional and the unspoken is now uttered. Over the years the memory filters and rearranges facts and chronology, but what never changes are the feelings—the emotion felt at the time. The images and the smells and the sounds are as ripe now as they were then. This was *their* war. It was fought in their country, their town, their street, their home, their hearts, minds and bodies. Their experiences are singular.

This book acknowledges the courage, spirit and heroism of these women. Bravery is in the mind of the beholder rather than in the opinion of the person themself. For that reason alone this book is important for those that may have held deep fears about their conduct during the war. At last they may accept that they are women of great character—whether or not others approve or disapprove of what they did no longer matters. And more importantly, they may realise they are not alone. Thousands of New Zealand women will recognise and identify with their stories.

Much of the credit that these stories have been finally told is due to the interviewers who worked on the original oral history interviews on which the subsequent film interviews were based. It was their skill and sensitivity that enabled the women to talk. When to their astonishment and relief their interviewer did not fall over with horror at the revelations, they gained the confidence to continue and say more. By the time they came to be interviewed on film their frankness was at times disarming, even for those who thought they had heard it all before. But none of the women told their secrets in order to shock. It was a genuine desire to answer our questions truthfully and to make a factual account. It was a decision they made only after a great deal of thought. They have all reached the prime time of life when they are comfortable as women and secure about who they are—so now, the time is right.

Some stories echo, some mirror, others are unique. The theme of love stories was not our choice—they chose themselves. We hope as you read the text of these odes, you can hear the sighs and the laughter and you can see the facial tics and the arms flapping—all the non-verbal language that is not defined on the page. We have endeavoured to leave breathing space around the words and sentences so you can hear the silences, the hesitation and the quickening of the heart beat. Now fifty years later the silence has been broken and the stories are told. The secrets are secret no longer.

This whole project is due to the singular vision and determination of Gaylene Preston. She has a talent for knowing how to arouse the human spirit and to soothe the mind.

Judith Fyfe

Pamela Quill

(née Buchanan, formerly Rabone)

When war was declared on the radio, Pamela was having an ordinary day, helping her mother with cooking and sewing on the farm. Much to her parents' horror, her brother, Lindsay, who was down in Dunedin learning to be a doctor, threw that in and joined the air force. Aeroplanes were fairly new then and to fly was a pretty thrilling sort of thing. He went into service in the RAF and was shot down by the Germans over Albania.

Pamela grew up on a farm at Kairanga on the outskirts of Palmerston North. Dancing, playing tennis and tennis parties—pre-war, it was a social, carefree life. Tomato soup and toast in town after the pictures was about as sinful as you could get those days. Even when the war started, life didn't change greatly; if anything war merely added a zest to what Pamela felt was already an exciting life.

He came into the room, and I just looked across at him. My heart started thumping, I felt sort of peculiar in the tummy, I felt weak at the knees. I thought he was just the most marvellous-looking being I'd ever seen and hoped like mad that he'd ask me to dance.
And I was sort of looking at him, but trying not to, because you know it wasn't really right to be too brazen about it all. But then to my amazement he came over and asked me to dance. Well of course I could scarcely stand up. I was in such a state of utter joy and thrill and we danced . . . we just sort of floated around. It was just the most wonderful sensation and I always felt more or less like that every time I saw him. He just had that effect on me.

    The second time, we went out together, chaperoned by my brother, he asked me to marry him and of course I couldn't believe this marvellous boy would want to marry me. And I remember going home and saying to my parents that I'd met the boy I was hoping to marry, and they said, 'Oh yes dear. Mm, how very nice'—they didn't believe it for a single moment. I was 17 and he was 19. He was my life. My whole existence depended on him.

It never occurred to me—there was no thought about not going to marry Paul. Because he was just so special and so totally different from anybody else I met.
He was always perfect. And as we got to know each other,

Paul at air force training, Wigram, 1938

20

I got to love him more. When we eventually did get together we were very, very happy.

By the time I met him, 1938, he was at Wigram. He had signed up for a short service commission and learnt to fly. Then he went to England and joined the air force. And so there was no question of my agreeing, or disagreeing, as to whether he should go. But in any case it wouldn't have made any difference. He would go. This is what he wanted to do, and he wanted me to go over there and get married, and I was quite sure that I would. It *never* occurred to me that I wouldn't be able to. He was always writing, 'Please come over, because I need you.'

My parents were absolutely marvellous—this is how wonderful—they were to help me to go to England.

My father knew the family, and felt that Paul was a fine young man and he would look after me and so on. And so I went to, I think it was External Affairs at the time, and told them that I wanted to go to England and get married—which was a pretty feeble sort of excuse I suppose, but to me it wasn't, it was very important—and they said, 'No, you can't go. Nobody's allowed out of the country.' I thought that they would say, 'Yes of course.' Anyway they didn't.

My father's response was, 'You must go to the top. Go to the Prime Minister.'

And I said, 'Oh my goodness he wouldn't be interested in me.'

Pamela, 1941. Spencer Digby Studios, Wellington

'Well,' he said. 'That's what you've got to do.'
I'd been trying for about six months and he was the last one to ask. So my mother and I, we made an appointment to see Mr Fraser, Peter Fraser.
I just didn't know what he was going to say and I thought that he might be very severe with me and tell me I had no right to do these things. We were ushered into his office and he was a very benign-looking man. He was a lovely man, really sweet and really nice, but to me, from Kairanga, the Prime Minister was something, you know, way up there and terribly, terribly *important*. He made us feel completely at ease and gave us a cup of tea and so on. And he wanted to know how long I'd known Paul and how I met him and how long we'd been separated. Paul had been flying in the, battle *for* Britain which I prefer to say instead of *of*.
And so Mr Fraser said that he felt that these boys deserved some sort of reward for saving Britain and in this case I would probably be Paul's reward. And so, yes, I could go.
I couldn't believe it. And he arranged with External Affairs permission for me to leave.

You got special treatment from the Prime Minister and yet this was wartime, people were suffering, there was loss and here you were in pursuit of a boyfriend?

Yes. I think probably my parents' contemporaries thought how stupid this was, and that I should behave myself and stay at

home. But the young ones thought it was all frightfully exciting. And I remember them, as I was leaving on the train from Palmerston North, and they brought down streamers and balloons and I sang 'Wish Me Luck As You Wave Me Goodbye'! And then I was off to Wellington to get on the *Mariposa*.
I just took one suitcase because I thought at the time, and still do, that it's better to have what you can carry without being dependent on other people.
So I just had my wedding dress, which was very important and was quite beautiful. Just a short dress and coat in a dove grey with white beading and a pale grey fox fur collar, made by Madame Fleck of Kirkcaldies—it was quite gorgeous. And of course, I took a wedding cake. Because you couldn't get wedding cakes in Britain. You couldn't make a cake in Britain, so I took my wedding cake with me, and whatever else was necessary.

    I got as far as New York and things went very sour.
They certainly did. Friends of the family from Palmerston had arranged for me to stay at the Roosevelt Hotel with a Dr Ross-Duggan, the resident doctor, and his wife. I understood that I was staying there as their guest, but, at the end of the week, I found to my horror that I was *charged* for my room. This of course took all my money.
My father had arranged for me to fly from New York to England but you had to fly to Lisbon first and then fly up to England, so I went to the Portuguese Consul, who said, you have to have a hundred pounds in cash before you can get out.

I was in a desperate situation with no money.
There I was stranded. I must get a job. But having been trained in nothing, apart from cooking and housework, I couldn't get one. I went round to try and wash dishes, anything at all, but they wouldn't take me on because I didn't have a permit. Eventually, I ended up at the British War Relief Society and told them my story.
Well, they were very angry that I had been allowed to leave the country. Allowed to get into this predicament. But anyway, they gave me $15 a week for packing bundles for Britain. I had to pay twelve and a half dollars a week at the hostel, so that left me two and a half dollars a week to live on. Which was a bit tricky. I had a roof over my head but a lack of food. With that two and a half dollars a week, I could have a milkshake a day and that was sort of reasonable.
But I had to save up a hundred pounds. I didn't want to ask my parents for any more money. I have no idea how they gathered together enough money to let me go, and so the thought of asking them for more money was totally out of the question.
I was getting pretty desperate.
    New York, for a young girl, really is a terrible place. The men come along and grab your arm and sort of walk you along. 'Come along with me honey.' People in open cars, the most marvellous-looking cars, would come along and say, 'Why don't you get in honey, I'll take you for a ride.' And of course they probably would have! But there was a taxi driver

who every day came along saying could he take me somewhere.
'You're not from New York, where are you from?'
And I'd say, 'It's none of your business.'
In the end I said I was from New Zealand. Yes, he thought I was from another country. And he said that he thought I was getting very thin and he'd like to take me for a meal.
I didn't think that was a very good idea at all, but I was getting pretty hungry so I went with him. He was probably in his 40s or 50s and he asked me what I was doing and I said I was going to marry a boy in England, and so on. And he took me down to the waterfront.

    I was quite convinced—white slavery was the thing—I'd had it. Never again would I see anybody.
We went to a little café with thick, brown, filthy curtains, down at the bottom of this long narrow place and as we went in the curtains were parted just a little bit and a face appeared. I was convinced that I was going to be shipped off somewhere—and he said, 'Give the girl a feed.' And so this man came out and he gave me a lot of food and I ate the lot in about two minutes and then, the taxi driver took me back to Allerton House.
And for the next several weeks, every day he would pick me up and take me to the café and I would have a meal. He was marvellous. Absolutely marvellous. I can't imagine what I would have done without him.

The extraordinary thing about that New York taxi driver is that I never knew his name.
I've thought since it was quite amazing that I didn't ask his name.

    I could see that I wasn't going to get anywhere near my goal of a hundred pounds so my future in-laws, Paul's parents, knew Sir Leonard Isitt who was in charge of the New Zealand Forces in Canada. They said, 'Get in touch with him,' if I was in trouble. So I wrote to him and he was very angry that I'd been allowed to leave the country. Really furious. Because I was taking up space which could be used for food or clothes being sent to Britain.
I didn't feel guilt. Not in the slightest. I'm afraid I was young and it didn't occur to me that I was doing anything terribly bad and I'm sure the amount of food that would have gone into my space wouldn't have amounted to that much, really. Somebody said, in fact several people, suggested I should go back home. I certainly wasn't going to go back home having got that far. I'd do anything at all to get to Paul. It was hair-raising, but it made me even more determined.
So anyway Sir Leonard pulled a few strings and then of course, everything fell into place.

Well, eventually I arrived in London and booked in at the Strand Palace Hotel because I was told, that's where all New Zealanders went to stay. And I rang Paul.
He was at a station about 30 miles out and he wasn't there.

They said he was away flying. So time went by . . . three hours went by, and he still hadn't rung me, and I thought, well, if that's what he thinks, I'll go out and have a look at this place. I was just going out . . . and standing in the foyer, when in he strode.

And once again—*ooh*—I thought he was the most marvellous person I'd ever seen and we just flung ourselves at each other and wrapped around each other, and stayed there I think it must have been for five minutes. All that time—it hadn't melted away. It was just so fabulous to see him.

And he said he must get me out of there. Why? And he said, 'It's full of pro's.' And I said, 'What are they?' The girl from Kairanga just was so naïve and so innocent.

Anyway he took me along to the Berkeley Hotel where we danced to Harry Roy and his band down in the restaurant and that was fabulous.

Did you spend the night together?

No. Goodness no. No he was in one room and I was in another. I should think probably quite a lot of people would have got together but, well, you know, my upbringing and absolute terror—I really, even then, didn't know anything about life, about sex. Probably he was the one who was quite magnificent in holding himself in check, as it were.

He said, 'Well we'll get married tomorrow.'

The next night I stayed with the local vicar and his wife so

Pamela and Paul, England, 1941

that was nice and safe, and the next day we were married. So I arrived in England on the 10th of September and we were married on the 12th at the Hunsdon Parish Church.

But they, the vicar and the wife of our best man who was an English girl, they wouldn't let me wear my wedding outfit. In England everybody was in uniform 'and only *actresses*' (said with total derision) wore those sort of things.
Of course Paul should have supported me but he didn't. He didn't care so long as we got married.
So I wasn't allowed to wear my beautiful wedding dress after all the trouble my poor little mother went to. It makes me angry every time I think about it actually, this pompous horrible attitude, just for my one special day. The vicar couldn't marry me unless I wore something plain and simple. So I wore a suit.
And then the boys in the mess decided that they must really, really celebrate my coming over there, and the wedding party, so they produced 'black velvet' which of course I'd never heard of. And we had the wedding cake, which was a tremendous success. So we had lots of fun and dancing, and one thing and another. It was all an absolute dream. I just, wafted through it because I was with Paul and we were in heaven.

We travelled about the country wherever he had to be in relation to his flying. As I said, 48 hours on and 48 hours off, so during the 48 hours off, when we were living in Kent, we'd go and sit by the riverside and eat cherries or go and see friends. There was a country club . . . we used to swim . . . you

could play tennis and so on. Because you didn't know what was going to happen tomorrow, we sort of clutched each other all the time
and I sometimes wonder how it would have been if it'd been just a normal, peacetime relationship because there was always this, rather urgent, feeling that maybe this was going to be the last time and so we must make the absolute most of it. Live for the day because we did not know what was going to happen tonight or tomorrow. He was a nightfighter pilot so I couldn't be certain if I cooked a meal if he'd be home to eat it. War took away the predictability of life. I am a fatalist now because I feel that covers up all the unpleasantness.
It wasn't a normal life although people tried to make it normal, it really wasn't.

When I had Penny I went to live in Sussex with a friend, another New Zealand girl whose husband was in the navy. (He was under the water and Paul was in the sky so there was always a lot to chat about.) We shared a cottage there because I really needed to be in one place having a baby.
Paul was then stationed at a place in Norfolk, called Little Snoring, and he flew down and stayed when he had leave for ten days, which was absolutely blissful. We agreed that we couldn't possibly be happier and life was just marvellous,
and he went back on the 22nd of July, and on the 24th I got a telegram to say that he was missing.

It just never occurred to me that anything would happen to him—he always used to say, 'Don't worry about me, I'll be

Paul and Pamela at the country club, 1942

alright, even if I get shot down I'll be alright,' and so on.
He was one of those people who always seemed to get out of
scrapes and problems . . . I knew he was in danger, all the
time, but I had this enormous confidence in his ability to get
out of whatever he got into . . . it *never* occurred to me that he
wouldn't turn up. So when the telegram came that he was
missing it seemed that he would reappear. He was going to
come back.

    The telegraph man on his bicycle came to the gate and he
came in and said he had a telegram for 'Mrs Rabone'—
something we always dreaded because invariably it was
something like this. Amabel was in the kitchen or somewhere,
and she immediately came out and sort of gave me a little
hug. I looked at the telegram, and it said he was missing.
We looked at each other and as she felt the same way about
Paul, that nothing could really happen to him,
we went in and had a cup of tea. Nothing very dramatic.

Then they kept saying, did I want to go home? Well I didn't
want to go home because I thought, if I went home, if he came
back, I wasn't going to be there.
New Zealand House, in the end, said that if I didn't go I
wouldn't get a free ride back home. It was a dreadfully hard
decision.
Dreadfully hard. Because as I say, I felt I was walking out on
him, deserting him, and I just hated it. But I had no money
and I was living in a house that had the drawing room

Paul playing with Penny while on leave, 1944

bombed off, so I did it, I came back on the *Rangitata* with Penny. It was the last troop ship from Britain and there were 1200 on the ship which normally took about 250, I think. They were really, really packed in, but it wasn't too bad.
I kept pretty much to myself and I had Penny, who was then three. She was a great joy.
I'd left New Zealand full of optimism and expectations . . . my dreams were going to come true.
Coming back—the arrival, was pretty awful. They put up, I don't know what you call them, sort of a gangplank I think it was called, not a gangway, a gangplank. It was really a very thick board, you know? And it had little slats that went across, every so often, and then instead of having a rod they had rope, so it was very unstable. I looked at it and said surely we don't have to go down this. 'Yes you do, yes you do.' I thought I might fall off.
I had my suitcase and Penny, so I sort of crouched down and told her to get on my back and put her arms around my neck and hang on whatever happened.
She says she remembers, even now, the fright, the alarm about it all. And then, I saw a slight shadow and I looked up and there was my marvellous darling father, and he said, 'It's alright darling, I'll look after her.'
He was a big man, a very strong man, and he managed to take her down this dreadful gangplank, and I was able to go down on my own.

    There were lots of hugs and kisses and tears and so on, and

Pamela and Penny, c.1944

then they took me back to the farm. So I'd had the complete circle, from the farm back to the farm.
But I couldn't live there—I'd been through too much, and they just didn't understand me. And so I went down to Wellington, by that time Penny was four and a half, and got a flat in Hawker Street.
That was very, very lonely really because I didn't know anybody in Wellington. I'd reached the stage where I couldn't stand men. They seemed to think a widow was *dying* to get into bed with them, and I wasn't the least bit dying to get into bed with them. I was still quite sure that Paul would turn up somewhere but I liked going out, instead of staying at home all the time. I enjoyed going out and having a drink somewhere and going to a party and so on, but I wanted to come home completely intact.

When I met Stan, at a friend's place, he was just so wonderful and he said he'd like to see me again—could he ring me? I said, 'Yes, that would be nice,' and so he invited me for lunch—at Kirkcaldies I think, or somewhere like that, and then he asked me to the air force ball.
At that ball, or after the ball, he asked me if I would marry him and I said, yes, I would because he couldn't have been more different from Paul. He was a lovely, quiet, nice man—somebody I really needed at that time. Somebody to lean on and depend on.
And he was, and always remained so.

I didn't hear for nine years what had happened to Paul. By then I was married to Stan and we were at Wigram and the Air Member for personnel came down visiting.
We were having a cup of tea, and I said to him, 'I'm surprised that Paul's name isn't on the Runnymede Memorial.'
And he said, 'Why should it be?'
And I said, 'Because he has no known grave,' and he looked at me, and said, 'Paul was found.'
No he didn't say 'Paul was killed' or anything, he said, 'But Paul was found.'
And you can imagine, I felt somewhat faint,
because you can imagine all the things that went through my mind then. Was he found dead or alive? Had he gone mad? Had he decided he didn't want to see me any more? Was I bigamist—was he still living somewhere? Was he with somebody else? What had happened? And the personnel man was sort of looking at me in a very perplexed way saying, 'But I thought you knew.'

    I didn't know. I'd never heard.

    When they sent the letter to say he was 'Missing in action. Presumed dead', that had been sent to an address where Amabel and I had been. This was just after the war. The people in that house hadn't seen fit to return the letter to Air Ministry so it was just that little quirk of fate that made it that I didn't hear. I didn't know that he was missing presumed killed, officially.
I think really the only time when I really knew that Paul no

longer was somewhere in the world was when I saw his grave in Belgium. Seeing his name there in this beautiful, beautiful area in the Ardennes—it really is lovely—it's nice, nice to know that he's there.

In 1946, Pamela, a war widow, returned to New Zealand, and two years later married Stanley Quill, who was in the RNZAF. With him she was posted to various air force stations in New Zealand as well as to Britain and Germany; during this time they had two children. In 1955 she finally made the pilgrimage to Belgium to see Paul's grave in a small war cemetery at Hotton.

Both Pamela and Stan shared a hatred of war and a bitterness toward those such as the ammunition makers who promote wars, so that they can make money. In 1984 they planned to go to Belgrade, where there was to be a meeting of military people from all over the world. The object of the meeting, which was instigated in Moscow, was to get together to discuss what could be done to stop wars. They were due to leave when Stan suddenly died.

Paul's grave in a small war cemetry, Hotton, Belgium

Doreen Foss
(née Lea)

Doreen Foss was an innocent schoolgirl in Featherston at the beginning of the war and a married woman with a baby at the end of it—still in Featherston. In between she was a cook and a cleaner and did 'all sorts of things'. At 15 she had her first job as housemaid on one of the big established farms in South Wairarapa. After 'a flaming row' with her mistress she was ordered out. This meant a move over the hill to the capital city where she had no trouble getting a job as housemaid, and eventually graduated to cook, at the Karitane Hospital in Melrose (a hospital specialising in the care of new babies and sometimes their mothers). She was uprooted from Karitane by the Manpower Commission to go and work as a landgirl.

What happened to Germany during the Hitler time I feel can happen to any country in the world. Here is one man like Hitler who gets up and he brainwashes millions of people because they allow it.

We had an old radio, it was one of the first ones down there and all we got was Parliament. Because Dad was very keen on Parliament you weren't allowed to listen to nice 'Count of Monte Cristo' or something like that. Politicians were talking, and he'd be saying, 'Sssh, there'll be a war, same as last time, there'll be a war.'
And it was jammed at you day after day after day at school also. When you're about 14, or something, you didn't even know what a war was. School was very patriotic then. You lined up in the morning and saluted the flag for a start-off then you marched into school with 'Colonel Bogey' or something like that. In class you all stood up and said 'God Save the King' and sat down.

The Germans were just some mysterious nuisance-makers. I don't think anybody that I know really hated the Germans. People say they did but I mean we wouldn't have known what a German was. I think a few of the boys used to draw up pictures about what they thought a German looked like with big teeth and tails and that sort of thing, on them. But no, we didn't hate them. They were just something in the background that was going to cause a lot of trouble.

But the Japs, that was different. Nobody liked the Japs. They were closer. We knew on the map where Japan was,

didn't we—they were too close. If they hadn't had the A-bomb it would have gone on and on and a lot more people would have been killed.
I think it was the best thing that ever happened. What's a bomb? It's no worse than a mountain going off and killing people, is it?

About '43 or '44, '43 it must have been, I'd turned 18 and I was working in a hospital. By then I was the cook.
My name must have been on the manpower list and I was manpowered to a farm at the back of Greytown.
They just sent you a notice and allotted you a job.
I should never have been taken out of there and put on a farm.
They didn't think that a cook in a women's hospital was as important as going and milking cows on a farm.
You must remember the women weren't very important.
    Well, I had to tell Matron all about this and she was quite indignant because she'd have to train up another cook.
Anyway, the next thing, I got told to turn up and pick up a uniform and some papers.
So I did. Skirt, pants, boots, gumboots, hat with a cocked-up side and flannel shirt. I was issued with a uniform and told to put it on. The coat was hanging down over me bum somewhere because I'm pretty small and these were standard clothes. I tried on a pair of gumboots and a pair of lace-up boots.
Me! I'd never worn anything like that before.

Anyway, I had to strut out of there all done up. I went back up to the hospital all dressed up to show the girls what I looked like. It's a pity somebody didn't take a photo. I only ever wore it once. So I picked up my bag and said goodbye to Matron and all the girls and everything. Came down, got on the train and the farmer was waiting for me at Featherston station to take me out to this place.
Funny enough I had never been along that road.
    I would be 18 and I'm on this farm—and of course I'm floored—I didn't know how to milk a cow. And as for chasing cows into bull paddocks I didn't know anything about that either. We had cows, but dad would never let me milk a cow. No. That wasn't my job.
Anyway, it was no trouble to work out how to put a machine on a cow, but the machines kept breaking down and you'd have to milk them by hand. There was about 40 cows. This farmer, he had plenty of cows and broken-down fences and machines that wouldn't go and he had a lot of land. They must have thought that he was doing good enough out of his cows to give him a landgirl.
    I had the meals with them in the kitchen and I had a bit of a room off the kitchen. It was very basic. There was no hot water and I remember trying to wash my clothes in cold water. That muddy cow mucky stuff, because the cows would shit all over you. Specially somebody that was fumbling round, who didn't know what they were doing.
And of course I eventually came out in cowpox all over. It

looks like chicken pox—scarlet fever sort of thing. It comes up in pustules. It was all over my face, all round my neck, all over my hands. I couldn't bend my fingers to get the machine twisted over to put it on the cow because of the sores.

Well the wife decided that it looked a bit suspicious so she carted me into the chemist at Greytown and I showed him all this and he said, 'Oh. You been playing with cows?'
I said, 'I haven't been *playing* with them I've been trying to milk them!'
And he said, 'You'd better get out of there, you're highly allergic.'

Anyhow, that's alright, I went back with the farmer and struggled on with the cows.
He'd say to me, 'A cow's jumped into the bull paddock. Go and get the cow out.'
I would say, 'I'm not going into anybody's bull paddock. You get your own cow out!'
You see I answered back. I wasn't going anywhere near a bull! So I'm looking at this joker and I thought, 'Yeah . . . ,' because you'd only have to get from here to there and he'd start this business, grabbing your backside business, to get his own back at me because I snapped. I'd duck if he made a grab at me.
He used to make me pick up the bobby calves and carry them down to the gate—instead of leading them down he made me *carry* them! Busted my boiler!

Anyway, this day it came to a head. He sent me way out the back—it would be about five or six paddocks over,

I suppose—and told me to pull a fence down. I don't quite know why. Anyway I got to work with the hammer and managed to pull this fence down. There was nobody there, there was a bit of gorse and a bit of fence.
Sure enough, he turned up alright. He appeared with a couple of dogs around the gorse. I don't know how long he'd been there. He must have followed me I suppose.
And he said, 'Oh you're not doing a bad job there,' or something of that nature, and just went grab. Just grabbed me. Here's me standing there with a hammer. I whacked him around the shoulder. Bang down on the ground I went. *Oomph*. He jumped on me but he didn't get anywhere though.
Well I kicked up like—gave him fingernails, a few kicks and knees and things and I screamed and yelled and clawed and he let me go. And he told me I was a little bitch that I knew too much and I said, 'I am going to go and tell your wife,' which I did.
Well she told me that I egged him on. It was my fault.

I suppose he was a frustrated man—but he had a perfectly good wife and a young kiddie about six months old.

So Jim turns up that night or the next night or whenever on his old Harley Davidson—
I'd known Jim then for about two years—and I told him all about this. And he says there's only one thing to do—'Come and see mum.' His mother lived in Carterton so I got on the back of the motorbike and off we go.
Gee that was a different story. Did she go mad!

Jim in the meantime had gone to the policeman, Andy Gregor in Greytown, told him about this and asked, 'Can she leave?' Andy Gregor said, 'Yes, but she'll have to go to the Manpower,' and he told Jim, 'Don't hit him or I'll lock you up.'
Anyway Jim's mother come to the rescue—mother and father pulled up in their old car and took me to Masterton to the Manpower joker there. She told him that if I had to stay there, there'd be trouble. She'd cause trouble.
'Oh well,' he said, 'you can go home. We'll be in touch. We'll never send another girl there.'
And so that was that.

I never got paid. I didn't get a bean and I was there a couple a months. I never got *anything*. I never got an apology from anybody and I never heard another word about the Manpower. I got the bus home and dad and my stepmother and my brother were standing there and dad said, 'And what do you think you're going to do? I'm not keeping you.'
It was *my fault* you understand.

I presume that farmer, he wanted to put another fence up there. I presume that's why he told me to go and do that. Now if he wanted to put a fence up why not put it there by the house? Not miles away down the back. And there wasn't anybody there. Looking back on it . . . I've never ever said anything about this to anybody—the only person I ever told was Jim and Jim's mother—but I did feel uncomfortable. I felt as if I'd been set up—but remember in those days you were innocent—I was uncomfortable. I kept looking around all the

Jim Foss with his parents, Featherston, 1939

time and wondering, 'What the hell am I doing here?'

While I was struggling, 'I'll tell your wife, I'll tell your wife.' If I hadn't said that I think he would have ripped my clothes off. Luckily you had overalls on—which was a thing you didn't wear in the 40s—nice girls didn't wear pants. That was quite good because otherwise I think he would have raped me. I had to cover that up. I wasn't allowed to tell anybody about that. I never ever told a soul why I was suddenly there then gone, back doing housework again. Dad would have murdered me if I had said anything. It was *my fault*.

Jim didn't think it was my fault. And my stepmother didn't think it was my fault. Thank god for stepmothers. His father just sniggered, so I don't know what he thought. Jim come along and I picked up my bag—I had a lovely ship picture on the wall above my bed and I left it there—I climbed out the window in the dark. Climbed on the back of his motorbike and disappeared in the middle of the night. Huh! Climbed out the window.

In time Jim and me got engaged. There was no point in getting married, because you had nowhere to live and you couldn't work and be married. That probably would have been easiest way out—to have got married out of that Manpower. They would have chucked me out anyway.

We were terribly bossed. I mean you couldn't go anywhere. You couldn't go across the road unless you had a nanny hanging around you. It was terrible. It was bad in the country.

When I was at Karitane there was six sisters and they used to take us to dances on Saturday night in the van. The driver—Leslie Davis was her name—took us into the hall and left us there. And after the dance was over she'd come back and escort us out and put us in the van.

If you poked your nose out the door there was trouble. But of course that didn't stop anybody having trouble, did it? But that's how they watched you.

Wellington, of course, it was blackout then. You weren't allowed to walk down the hill from Melrose and get some fish and chips by yourself. Whether they thought the bogey man was going to jump out of the bushes I don't know.

One of the girls that was working at Karitane, Billy, was pretty good at raking up gents from somewhere—and I can't even remember what his name was, but anyway, I had to go to the pictures with him. (Gee I got teased over that too. Those girls gave me a hard time about that—because they knew about Jim hovering in the background.) Anyway I met this joker and we went to the pictures and had some fish and chips. But there was nobody to take me up the hill. My escort had let me down.

So he proceeds to walk me up the hill and it was a bitterly cold day I can remember and he had his greatcoat over his shoulders and he said, 'You want to watch this you know,' he said, 'I might try to dirty dick and duck behind one of these bushes,' and suddenly I realised, 'That's what Matron's frightened of.'

Karitane Hospital domestic staff, Featherston, 1942.
Doreen is on the left

We went into shrieks of laughter. But you know, I could never make out why Karitane was playing godmother—in my innocence, I thought *I* was important.
They were just looking after you!

To be quite honest I haven't really got any feelings about the war at all.
No, the only nuisance was getting manpowered onto that farm. If I'd have stayed in Wellington, I would never have married Jim and probably I would have had an entirely different life. You've got to look at it that way.
　You see, those stupid men really ruined it in a way because I think that from that hospital I would have gone on alright. I had enough brains to know what I was doing. I could have done anything. I could have been a very clever cook for a start off. Which although my brother sneers at it, cooks make a lot of money.
Never in my life would I have gone back to Featherston if I hadn't had to. Because when you live in a little place like that, the big city's where you wanted to go.
But I had to go back—they sent me back. So instead of that I ended up in Featherston didn't I, and I'm still there.

Doreen and Jim on their wedding day, 7 March 1944

Doreen and Jim Foss married in March 1944. After her first child was born she continued to work at her job cleaning the local primary school. The daily impact of war hardly affected her, except for minor irritations. She recalls, 'The butter rationing got up my nose. Alright, it went to the war effort, but I think there was enough butter for us to have our share. That annoyed me.'

In some ways life today is even more frustrating; she is no longer able to get on her bike and go down the road. She and Jim are pretty thoroughly retired now, still living in the same land they moved onto over 50 years ago.

Doreen is convinced that her fate was sealed by the war. It wasn't just a matter of what happened to her—it was more the fact that other people made decisions for her. Not ones that she would necessarily have made for herself.

Tui Preston

(née Macdonald)

This is a portrait of a wartime marriage. Tui was a young wife and mother, married in August 1940 during the war. Her husband was overseas with the armed forces for nearly five years (or as Tui recites: 4 years and 178 days). She was a virtual widow for much of that time.

Tui grew up and married in Greymouth. She was raised in an extended family situation by a solo mother. There were two sisters and two brothers in her immediate family.

She was told on her thirteenth birthday that she had to go to work because her mother could not afford the uniform that was necessary for high school. She didn't mind, because she was used to being told what was going to happen and accepted that it was necessary.

For nearly ten years, up until the war, she earned her living in a variety of jobs, including shopgirl in a furniture retail store, saleswoman, tearoom attendant and cake decorator. She stopped work shortly before the birth of her first child.

Until her marriage when she was 24, Tui had lived at home in a very small, overcrowded house. She shared a bed with her sister Mavis. It was a sisterhood of sharing in a frugal household. The three girls vied for the communal supply of shoes, undies and stockings. Tui recalls it was a case of one pair on, one pair in the wash and one pair in the drawer. Stockings were dried overnight on the oven door (in the oven sometimes!) or as often happened one sister took the dry pair and left the wet. It was a case of first sister up, best dressed, in the Macdonald household.

Despite the financial constraints of the family, Tui has warm memories of the short time she had as a young woman in the 1930s. Apart from work, her life consisted of family gatherings and the church, and her pleasures were sewing, music and dancing.

I loved music and I loved to cavort around in my own way, and when the radio came in I just adored it. I really got to like dancing. We'd go to granny's place and someone would play the piano and the family'd dance, and quite often an uncle or aunt would take one of us and show us a few steps of a waltz. Ooh I just felt in another world, just as though I was wafting off into the sky, my whole body and mind was part of the dance. It was perfection.

'Tui in her Easter bonnet', 1942

I always *loved* dancing.

When I got to Bible class, that's when I learnt to dance properly because we'd have socials, and it was a law, an unwritten law, that the first man who came and asked you, for the dance, 'May I have this dance please?',
even if you wanted someone else in the hall to come to you, you didn't say no, you just got up with him, and if he couldn't dance, well you just did it and taught him a few things.

It was all very, very lovely, nice, smooth. You never got angry because you didn't get a dance with the one that you liked to dance with best.

They used to have a ladies' choice—one ladies' choice in the evening—and you could see all these ladies lined up ready to make a beeline for the best dancer . . . race across the hall to this one that you particularly wanted to dance with because he was a great dancer.

You never went out of the hall. Never went out of the hall. The ones who went out of the hall and came back, they were bad girls, 'hussies' who didn't care.
At first I didn't know what that really meant but you just were told by your peers that you didn't leave the hall at any stage. And you never went home with anybody who just said, 'Can I take you home?', until I got older and then it was people I knew.
They'd say, 'Oh I'll accompany you home,' and that's all it was. Just walked you home and chatted and said goodnight and

Tui, 16 years old, 1932

that was it. There was no romance of any kind in it.

My mother and I used to go and play cards at a friend's house
and I met a young man there,
well he was much older than me. I was only about 16
and one night my mother didn't come and play cards at this
house and he was there as usual, and the lady of the house,
Mrs Maguire, she said, 'Well you can take Tui home tonight,'
and he walked me home and I was quite attracted to him.
I didn't know what that word 'romance' meant even at that
time, but I just sort of felt, that's nice, when he took hold of
my hand and we walked hand-in-hand and I can still
remember how I felt . . . 'This is so unfamiliar. It's different,
it's nice . . . mmm.'
And he did that two or three times when he walked home with
me and then one night he kissed me and,
I can't explain how I felt about all this different feeling I had,
just through our lips touching. And it was, it was . . . oh it was
different.
And then when I got home, I worried, I thought oh my
goodness I'm going to be pregnant, because I shouldn't have
felt like that. I just hadn't a clue. I didn't know *anything*.

    I was a prudish girl. Didn't want to know.
Girls would be talking in the corner, this was when I was older
at these dances (when we went into the ladies' room, to
powder our nose or whatever it was),

and these little clutches of girls around whispering away and
you could join it and listen if you wanted to. But oh, no, *I*
didn't want to hear that—that was *dirty talk* about their
boyfriends.
I was terrible. I can't believe that I was like that!

Young men didn't drink so much in those days. But during the
dances, a group of them, a certain number of them, of which
Ed was one, they'd go outside and have some beer.
If it was the Blaketown Dance there was a bush at the back
and they used to go out there and have their drinks.
Well I loved dancing with Ed. I knew him for a long time but
just as a brother more or less, and he would come in and I'd
know that he'd been outside and he'd come over and he'd say,
'Will you have this one?'
I always think of Ed as different to anyone else, absolutely
different. And I'd stand up and I'd say, 'Breathe on me,'
because as I say he was like my brother. And he'd look at me
and clamp his mouth closed and I'd say, '*Breathe on me,*'
and I can smell it you see, and I'd say, 'No I'm not dancing
with you, you've been drinking.'
And I just stuck to it. And he would make some funny remark
and go off and stand down the end with the fellas and you'd
hear a shout and a hoot with these chaps laughing about him
being turned down.
But that chap of mine, he got cunning.

He used to have these little pink . . . not peppermint, they were used for making the breath smell nice . . . aniseed . . . he used to have these in his pocket even if he hadn't had a drink (it got to the stage where I didn't know whether he'd been drinking or not).
And he used to take my hand while we were dancing and put it in his coat pocket like that and give my hand a little bit of a tickle while I was in there taking out one of these wee aniseeds. And that became a habit, as soon as I got up for a dance with him, I'd always have to put my hand in his pocket.

Ed was a good dancer, but he wasn't good enough for me, if you know what I mean. I needed to learn new steps and I was a light person and I liked to sort of jump with the rhythm but he didn't. He was solid on his feet.
But he was a beautiful waltzer and it got to the stage that he'd say, 'Keep the last dance for me and I'll have the maxina waltz.' Didn't matter about the rest.
He'd tell me this when I came into the hall and they were always, right up till we stopped dancing, they were always *his* dances.

I felt beautiful when I danced . . . oh I did . . . I felt like a princess.
I always made a new ball frock because I loved to sew, I always designed my own and I even got my name in the paper. You know how they used to have about debutantes and 'such-and-such a ball was held'?

Ed with his pet spaniel, 1939

I think this was a Radio Ball later in life, and I'd made this dress—it was daffodil yellow, moray taffeta with lovely big puffed sleeves—nice, nice shapes. And I had a Dorothy bag made out of purple velvet hanging on my arm. And I was given a write-up in the paper. I thought that was wonderful.
I loved going to a ball and dressing up and going to a dance, always was special. Getting ready to go.
Even getting ready to go to church is still . . . I feel different. I take time.

    We had a busy life. Church kept you very, very busy in the social events in your life. It wasn't all just religion.
And I enjoyed my job at the Harker's Tea Rooms. I started as counterhand and progressed to head girl, I learnt how to make and ice cakes.
It was a very happy time of my life.

When the war broke out it really wasn't a big deal as far as feeling, 'Oh, this is going to be dreadful. It's war.'
Greymouth was a very quiet compact place that had its own rules in many cases. So a lot of it didn't touch us, but when these young men started to talk about joining up—then it started to get interesting, particularly for mothers.
    Ed was down at our place having tea one night and he said, 'Well I've joined, I've joined to go overseas with the infantry, Mrs Mac.' (He always called mum 'Mrs Mac'.)
We all stopped dead. We always had family tea on a Sunday night, and there was always other kids there besides my

Head girl at Harker's Tea Rooms, Tui is standing to the left of Mr Harker, who is wearing a bow tie, Greymouth, 1939

brothers' and sisters' friends. The house was always full.
And he said, 'Yes I'm going and Jim Smith's going . . .' and
named all these buddies of his '. . . we're all going to go
together,' and he was full of it.
And then of course he didn't get called up for some time,
neither did the others, but they were making sure they were
all going to be going together.

    Finally they got a date. Well, by this time Ed and I had got
into a situation where, you know, we developed a relationship
and of course as it got nearer to the time for him to go away it
was really making us feel that this thing that had developed
between us . . . how were we going to cope?
And it gradually developed into a sexual relationship and at
first it was . . . we both, well me particularly,
I thought that it was dreadful that I had done this thing . . .
because it was the first time.
And I worried—never had anybody who I ever talked to about
anything—anyway it happened again and again and . . . some
time, I think it would be in, July, June, I knew that I was
pregnant.
I didn't tell a soul. I used to go to my room and worry and
think, is there anything I can do? I didn't even tell Ed.
And as for telling my mother that was the hardest part of all
because, she was everything to me. Had always been. She
brought us up on her own.
The thing that bothered me the most was that I'd let her down.
I *couldn't* tell her—but I did have to tell Ed. I knew I had to do

something about it as time was going on. And so we arranged to go down and tell mum.
I arranged it when none of the family would be there. Just mum and him and I.

I'll always remember it. It was, it was awful.
I'll never forget her face. And she didn't upbraid me but did she tell Ed off! She really did. He was sitting on the kitchen chair, just an ordinary kitchen chair, and she said, 'I took you into my house and you've let me down.'
Not *me*, she didn't say *I'd* let her down. But it was me, she was telling, indirectly. I figured that out.
And then, she said, 'Well, you're going to get married.'
Neither of us said no we don't want to because we just knew we had to. When I look back I don't think I even thought about wanting or not wanting to get married. At that particular time you had to. And the emphasis is on *had to*, there was no option. Your parents said you had to get married and you had to.
But certainly we weren't ready for it.

So that's how it happened about my pregnancy.
Mother took over from then and she wanted me to have a nice wedding with a white frock (which I designed myself), and all the trimmings and it just went from there.
In August we were married. I have hardly any recollection of that day. I only remember that I could see myself in the mirror above the mantelpiece standing there holding my bouquet looking absolutely desolate.

Tui on her wedding day, 21 August 1940

I've got a photograph of that and that's just how I look. It just wasn't me. I looked empty. Nothing there.

When I walked down the aisle Ed turned and looked back at me and he was white as a sheet. And that was the start of it. I don't remember much of the rest of the day. I just remember that we went to the reception, for the cutting of the cake—that was all we did—a few speeches and the cutting of the cake.
It was a real grand spread which my boss had put on for me because I worked in the tea rooms, cake shop, that he owned and they had a big reception room upstairs. My wedding was as grand as anybody else's.

And then we caught the train to Christchurch to have our honeymoon, as it was called, to stay with my aunt and uncle in Christchurch for a week.
We had five pounds between us I remember that. That's all we had. The train was called an express but it took five hours to get to Christchurch from Greymouth.
I don't remember much of the journey because I was really in shock I think, when I look back on it. Must have been. I didn't want to be in this situation . . . 'How did I get here?' . . . and was very, very uncommunicative all the way. And Ed was very quiet too—we just sat there.
When we got to Christchurch, Uncle Russell called for us and took us to the house. And they had given us the room with the double bed in it. And while I'd always slept in a double bed because my sister and I slept together, growing up . . . this was a *massive* thing . . . it was the biggest bed I'd ever seen and I

just . . . well I just went through the motions.
I think we both did.
I don't know if you want to hear this. But that night . . . my aunt was a very jolly sort of a person and she laughed a lot and loved a joke . . . and when we got into bed and started to settle down this bell rang underneath the bed. She'd put a tiny bell underneath. Ed thought it was funny but I was so upset. It seemed just sordid to me, you know? It was making a mockery of everything.
Maybe I had to have an excuse for the way I felt.
But when she came in the morning with a cup of tea on a tray for us and her face beaming, Ed said, 'You got up to some trick last night didn't you?' And I laughed but I didn't mean it. Didn't think it was a bit funny.

Ed had enlisted, right at the beginning. Then you found out you were pregnant and got married. Did he rethink about going away?

Oh no. No he didn't, because I asked him could he not defer it until after the baby was born. And he said, 'No, I've enlisted and I have to go—I've promised so-and-so . . . ' (names of the men who were his friends—his buddies) '. . . we want to go together.'
Mind you, all those boys who went away then they thought it was just going to be a hoot, that they were going to have a holiday at the expense of the country. See other countries.

They thought in weeks, months, nothing else.
Well, I wasn't a fierce sort of a person. I didn't tell him I thought he should go or he shouldn't go, but I was deeply hurt that he wouldn't even make enquiries about it and I always felt that I didn't come first.

Well, our lives continued for about six weeks in his mother's house and then he had word to say that he was to be in Burnham on a certain date.
And so the day came, and I just packed up and went back home to my mother.

Well I was fine and the pregnancy was fine and he kept coming home the odd weekend. And he had three final leaves, they kept procrastinating and altering the dates and this sort of thing.
We had these three final leaves and when he was going on the last one I said, 'Look if you get another one, please, don't come back. Just let them tell me you've gone.'
I couldn't have faced it, and neither could he. It got harder and harder each time saying goodbye because by this time we were very, very close. I was his world and he was mine, and he was going and I was staying.

Oh it was lonely. It was terrible.
It really was—it was awful. That was the only time in my life I've ever been alone until now. I wasn't living in a house alone—the family, friends, they couldn't have been more supportive,

Tui visiting Ed at Burnham Military Camp, 1940

Tui wearing Ed's army cap when he was on home leave, Greymouth, 1940

but I was alone. Just me.

That was a dreadful New Year's Eve after Ed went.
We always went to the Square, it was a tradition in those days. Everybody took whistles and banged things and jumped around like a lot of lunatics and enjoyed themselves, had fun, danced and everything.
I was standing there with all these people rooting around me and I started to cry. I felt that there wasn't anybody in the world who was interested in me—that I was alone in the world, and I just cried and cried.
My sister and brother said, 'Come on, we're going first footing,' and I said, 'No, take me home.'
The New Year meant that I had nothing to look forward to and I wasn't looking past tomorrow.
That was a dreadful part of my life.

Only once did I get upset about being pregnant and that was when the doctor said I had to go into hospital early to have the baby because I had problems.
My mother said, 'You'd better go and tell Ed's mother.'
It was late morning so I decided I'd walk up. I'd be quite big, you know, like thin people are, and I'd put on a very nice coat that I used to wear—a modern coat, not suitable for pregnancy. I was walking past the goods sheds and I heard this laughter.
It didn't worry me at first, but there was just me walking along this stretch of road, which just seemed like an eternity, and these men, hoons I'd like to call them, were calling to

each other, 'Come and have a look at a pregnant woman!'
And when I got to Ed's mother's place I was in tears crying. I couldn't tell her what had happened. It just seemed to me that I had been a figure of fun. Pregnant women were supposed to hide themselves.

When my baby was born, things changed so much and I was never alone again. He just took over my life.
I couldn't have managed without the help of my mother. She was a saint, she was wonderful and that boy right even to the time she died was just the apple of her eye.
My mother tried to get in touch with Ed when the baby was born. She tried to get in touch with someone who could let him know. The powers-that-be said there was no way they could tell anybody while they were in transit. So the first thing he knew about being a father, was when he got to Alexandria and the Maadi Camp. Someone who'd gone away with the 3rd Echelon before Ed, came racing down to him and said, 'Hello daddy!'
And the letters that came, from Maadi Camp when he was stationed there, were very brief and had lots cut out of them. Literally cut out with scissors.
All he told me was what he was doing . . . that he was on guard duty or playing poker with the boys or he'd gone out to see the pyramids and, you know made it sound as though he was having a high old time,
which he probably was.

He was taken a prisoner in November. They let me know—

a telegram from the Minister of Defence to say that he was missing.
Just, 'Regret to tell you that your husband, E J Preston . . .' blah blah '. . . is reported missing, in action.'
And that telegram came in the morning just as I was getting ready to go down to help my old boss at the shop.
I don't remember anything about the next few days. Didn't even know what happened to my little boy. I suppose I was in shock, maybe I was sedated as well. I can't remember.

   Waiting, waiting to hear what had happened, to him.
Well of course, I thought the worst—you do.
I've always been a worrier, worry is essential because it's a way of planning.
Well the next telegram said, 'Missing, presumed a prisoner of war.' Then waiting to hear where he was took ages.
Ages and ages.

   By that time, I was beginning to find that my child filled my life. I mean I still, I was still upset and, wondering all the time and waiting for that knock at the door to say the worst.
You do look for the worst, don't you, in these situations, well I did.
And it was some time before I got news through the Red Cross to say he was in a transit camp somewhere in Italy—
it was always 'somewhere'—and that he would be allowed to write to me in time.
Well it would be six months before I got the first one and it was just an open card which said, 'I am fit and well, how are

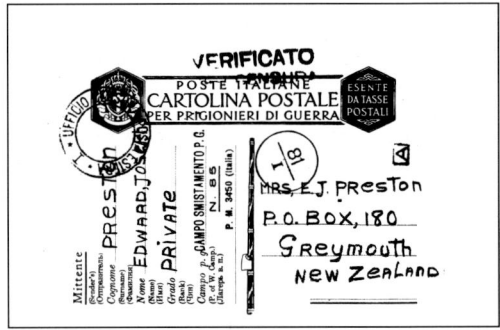

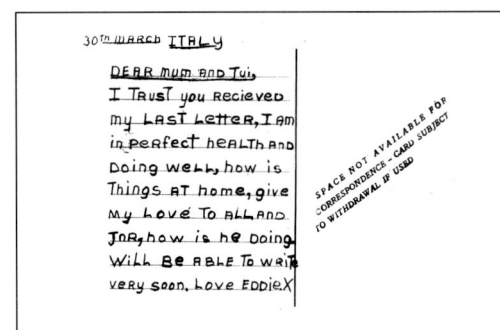

you?' Literally—just as though it was someone on holiday sending a quick word.
I expected another one perhaps with more information. But in all I only got about six, or it might have been less than that, all the time he was away.
That helped me to realise that . . . Ed wasn't here any more.
It was as though he was dead. That he just wasn't. I couldn't even bring a vision of him in my mind by that time.
They sent all his gear back. It took a year or two, but I got it in a rucksack. All his personal gear.
And his diary was in it—I looked through that diary and I couldn't find where he'd been told he was a father.
It was as though he'd cut himself right off. In order to survive, I suppose.
And that helped me too because I knew he didn't need me.

So as time went on, and no communication from him, I just picked up my life and I began to do the things that I'd always loved doing, apart from looking after my boy.
I got part-time work in the Borough Council office, research for the EPS, which was the emergency precaution services. There were local services that were set up to help if we were attacked. So my job was to find people to get into these units, like vehicles had to be impressed, lighting had to be under someone's supervision, all those things had to be controlled. Food, everything had to be under supervision in an emergency. It was run through the town hall

Photograph returned in Ed's kit bag, in which he had incorporated a photo Tui had sent him of herself and the baby, 1941

and I had my own room there and I used to type as I was a secretary once, and I used to do typing and bookkeeping and keeping the rolls in order.

I found it very, very interesting, and sometimes I could take my little boy with me and he would sit there and draw.

So it was great, I got a bit of social life back and with the family dos and get-togethers. It was the beginning of a new life for me. Another path.

I started going to dances. At first I felt a bit apprehensive. I thought they would think, 'Oh her husband's away and there she is enjoying herself.' But they didn't, I don't think. If they did I don't know about it.

I was going to dances and balls and meeting people, but always going in a group—there would be a partner for each person in the group. I never got involved with anyone of the opposite sex except as friends.

But I did get involved when I was at this job. This was a couple of years later after Ed had gone and as I said I never thought about him much. It was as though my life had changed completely. I was a mother and that made a difference of course.

And I had an affair, yes. It started out quite . . .

I knew him long before I was married, this was one of the ones who was a wonderful dancer and the one that I used to hope would come and, and dance with me . . . I didn't know him all that well but we got to know one another and he used to do all the modern dances and he taught me all the steps.

Tui, her grandmother, mother and baby Edward, Greymouth, 1941

When he used to ask me to dance it was a real honour because he was considered to be one of the best dancers around.

    Anyway, he was in charge of the appropriation of vehicles, so we worked together during the day, doing research and then sometimes we had to go and do checks at the Post Office at night. He would come to the house and pick me up because he had a car.

I suppose by the standards then, he was quite well off. Single and sort of an aloof person, not in our league at all. But we did these things at night and afterwards we would go to the milkbar outside the theatre and have our milkshake and he'd take me home and there was no secrecy about it.

I mean, I was seen to be going somewhere with this man but because there was nothing to hide in the relationship it was quite open and it never entered my head that anybody would think that I was having . . . but it did develop.

It started by him inviting me to come up to his flat and he'd put records on and we'd dance and that was all there was to it, for a while.

But then, it just developed into a sexual thing. And I did enjoy it with him . . . it was just . . . different. We got on very well and we could talk about lots of things, which I didn't do very well in those days with just anybody.

And he taught me to have confidence in myself. I had none. He was good for me. I don't think anybody can understand the way I felt . . . until they've done it . . .

because I had to pretend that he didn't exist, that there wasn't anything going on. Trying to hide something like that is awful. It does something dreadful to your mind, you're so conscious of it, all the time.

But it was a lovely relationship.
A separate part of my life that was totally different in every way. He was a totally different person to anyone I've ever known. I feel that that part of my life is quite a separate bit and I think that's helped me to sort of bury it and not feel so bad about it. Because I know it was good for me. I did need it, to grow up.
And I did grow up as far as sex was concerned, because I knew nothing when I got married and I didn't know anything when I got pregnant
and so, looking back on that it was a good thing that happened to me.

The relationship stopped suddenly when I got word to say that Ed . . . this was four years and 178 days after he'd gone away . . . and I get this word to say that he will be arriving in New Zealand (as usual no dates) and I would be notified later. So, my friend wanted me to make a life with him and never to go back to Ed, but I knew it wouldn't happen for the simple reason that I had a son.
And in those days, women had no rights whatever. I discussed it with my mother. She said be careful or you'll have your boy taken off you.
Of course that was just out of the question. I wouldn't even consider that and, if I had walked out on Ed, I would have

been the villain of course.

So out of the blue, another shock. Ed's return.

Yes. He rang—it was like a voice from the grave.
It was frightening.

What was that reunion like?

We met at the Christchurch railway station. I don't remember a lot about it. I just know that we were very polite to one another and he shook hands with the little boy because that was the way they did it in those days.
But the little boy was very reticent. (I keep saying the little boy, it was my son . . . our son.) And then the ride back through to Greymouth he showed quite plainly that he didn't like his father sitting beside me and holding my hand.
And then, that night I bought some pyjamas and a dressing gown in for Ed and our son said, 'Is that man staying at our house?' And I said, 'Oh, yes, it's your daddy, he's going to stay with me,' or something to that effect.
And then of course when I didn't come to sleep in his room I said, 'I'm going to sleep in the other room,' he said, 'Is that man going to sleep in your bed?'
And you know it was very hard to explain, I don't think I tried. I just said something like, 'Mummys and daddys do that.'
I had this repulsive feeling about sex when it came to knowing

Edward, aged 3, Greymouth

that I had to get into bed with this man who was a complete stranger, because we didn't know one another. It was just like we were meeting for the first time.
We were so out of touch.
And I'll never forget the first night we came to our house and mum had given us the room with the double bed in it, we sat up and sat up, and I think he was scared too when I look back. He got into bed first, I turned out the light and got into bed and I was so tense, I was way over on the other side of the bed and I thought, 'Oh, I can't go through with this.'
But he didn't touch me. He didn't touch me and I appreciated that. We didn't say anything. Couldn't talk about it. Nothing was said the next day.
We never talked about anything and so there was a rift there for a long time. We had a rocky time from then on.

    It wasn't just Ed—I was a different person. I'd grown up a lot, more than he had—he was really always a man's man, rugby, racing and beer—I was not just a wife, I was a mother too, which took over priority for me.
No, it was a very hard time for us but as far as the other relationship was concerned it stopped, like that. I just said no. I couldn't leave my child.
I regretted it ended. I was sad. I often used to find myself looking up the street when I was in the town hoping for a glimpse of him, like you do.
But I had enough to contend with, because Ed and I, we really didn't get on. He was very depressed, at times. He used to

disappear and come back and then I was depressed.
It didn't help matters that the little boy and his father didn't know one another. They resented each other. That complicated the situation so that we seemed to always be battling—opposing one another.
It was a really terrible time. How we got through it, I thank the Lord for it, because I'm quite sure I couldn't have done it if I hadn't had somebody or something helping me.

I think we just sort of stumbled through it and we settled down in time but it took years before we really got into a time of appreciating each other.
Putting up with each other for a start and then appreciating one another and there was such a lot that he gave to me, too.
He was a wonderful man really. He had different ways, but Ed was Ed. What you saw was what he was.
And we never went into long discourses and discussions about things.
I'd have been better if I could have said what had happened—if we could have discussed it—but he wouldn't. He didn't want to know.
So you didn't talk about it, it was a no-no. So I had to just work my way through that and no doubt he had lots to work through.
He was a prisoner a long time and he never talked about that either. I just wanted to know how awful it must have been for him but he said, 'Don't ask me about any of that, I don't want to talk about it', and he didn't.

Tui, Ed and Edward. Christmas Eve, 1945

But we got there. He was a good supporter.
And there's many many times that I'm sure he would have gone too because I must have been impossible to live with. But the battles got less and the nice side took over.
We got a rehab loan and we got our own house and I think, if there was a turning point . . . that was the beginning of it, of our, getting things together because, I've always been a homemaker. I love housework. I love being a homemaker, being with family, and taking them over. I worked on that. I kept myself busy.
And when Ed got the fish and chips business I used to go down for the busy periods and wrap up fish and chips while he did the cooking.
I think things became much easier because my mother came to live with us. She had a stroke and there wasn't anyone else who could have her in the family so she came to live with us and Ed never raised any objections.
And you know, they were the greatest of mates always. Mum adored him and he adored her.

 Ed and I became great friends—he was my mate and I was his. We looked after each other to the end and now I'm so pleased we had five lovely years, in our autumn years, when he got sick and I was given the heaven-sent ability to be able to look after him until he breathed his last in his own bed.
And that means everything.
It's made a difference.

 Even now, certain music will take me back to years ago

when I'd put my hand in Ed's pocket and take one of those little aniseed things out. They were put there for me, not always because he'd had a drink.

There's some songs that mean a lot to me, particularly when it's a waltz. He asked for one of them to be sung at his funeral—one that had deep memories for us of our early life together—that short time after we were married when it was lovely.

And often when we heard music, dance music on the radio, he would say, 'Come and have a waltz, mum,' and we'd be waltzing away in our living room.

Tui's and Ed's marriage was in many ways a great partnership—together they raised a family of three and ran several businesses. Part of their personal survival may have been the unspoken agreement that neither would talk about that time apart. Tui says she was never a communicative person—not even within her own family—and it took all these years to tell her story to another person. Because speaking openly about her past is so recent, she has never known whether other women held guilty, but important, secrets. She sometimes wondered whether she was the only one.

When I look back, those years were well worth all that. It shows me that everything's got to be fought for and to appreciate it it's got to be worth battling for. I think, at this stage of my life, that it was mostly for good. There was so

Tui and Ed

much happening to me, during the war years, I was sort of catapulted into development—made me grow up, be less selfish. I learned to take charge of my own life and cope with whatever came along. I think the war made women more independent and equal with men.

I've got to say that I've had a wonderful life really. My philosophy is that when it's been bad, it's 'history'—and if it's been good, it's 'memories'.

Jean Matekitewhawhai Andrews

(née Budge) QSM

'Auntie Jean' as she was widely known was married with two little girls at the outbreak of war. None of her immediate family was old enough to serve overseas but a number of her relatives were in the Maori Battalion.

The American invasion in 1942 was to have a long-term impact on her whanau. Their ancestral land at Paekakariki was acquired by the government of the day for camps for the servicemen. At the time of the interview the family was still negotiating to get it back.

The arrival of the American marines in her little village (population c.530) in the middle of 1942 changed their lives. 26,000 troops were stationed in the district and an extra 300 men were brought in to shovel coal, dig roads and provide services for the camps. Auntie Jean's husband, Paramahia Andrews, a truck driver for a local transport company, also got involved.

According to Auntie Jean, because the extended family was one of the few Maori families, and because they treated the Americans better than the Pakeha did, they became 'special to the visitors from Stateside'; many friendships made then remain to this day.

Paekakariki, c.1939. Beattie Collection, Alexander Turnbull Library

I'm Ngati Haumia hapu in Paekakariki. My tribal affiliation is Ngati Toa, I'm a direct descendent of Apihana Mutu Mira who originally was a chief at Paekakariki, at Wainui Pa. We have our own burial ground there. It's now Queen Elizabeth Park but the land originally belonged to Apihana Mutu Mira and his whanau.

We had a big old homestead there at Paekakariki, a five-bedroomed house with a big verandah around it which was demolished in late '39, because they were going to build an American camp there. So it was demolished—the old family homestead. Mmm.
There was no option there. It just happened . . . Public Works Department took over to build the American camp, in late '39. You had no option, they just did it.
Well you couldn't do nothing about it, it was wartime.

We were overrun by contractors building and carting coal . . . everything had to be there for these people. Camps just popped up everywhere, and the contractors all moving in—it was just a hive of activity . . . the village grew milk bars and

things that we never even knew about. All getting built in
a hurry.
We were just ordinary locals so all we had to do was prepare
for war work, whatever's to be done at the time.
The camp just grew and grew, and eventually the first lot of
marines arrive and Bob's your uncle . . . bang. Bang.

Not knowing how many people are going to arrive—came
the day that they did—my husband came rushing over and he
said to me, 'Get down by the pub there, and you'll see these
baboons arriving,' he said, 'trainloads of them.
They're starting to arrive at seven o'clock.' So I said, 'Alright.'
I told all the neighbouring . . . in those days the population
was quite small, so everybody knew everybody else's business
. . . so I told one person and she told the next one, so we ended
up nearly the whole village was congregated to watch out for
these people.
And the first train came in.
They poured out, little wee short things with their full
pack up.

And the thing that really struck me that morning was our
Trentham Military Band was there and they got the first group
to march all the way up to McKay's Crossing, imagine that,
with full pack on! And each group that come marching down
to the station, well I mean they couldn't march, they were
never marchers anyway, but they come slogging down with
packs on . . . soon as I see a dark one—looked like a Negro or

Jean standing in front of her husband, Paramahia
Andrews; among friends, 1940s

Mexican or whatever—clap, clap—I'd get my girls to clap . . .

    And that was about four o'clock in the afternoon.
Well we were so carried away watching all these different types of people, that we didn't even get hungry, you know?
And I said to my biggest girl, 'Run up home and make yourself a sandwich because Mum wants to watch what's going on.'
'No, I want to watch too,' she said.

    By the time the last train came in, it teemed with rain.
I rushed up home to light the fire for my two little girls and I, because me husband used to come home and have a meal and then go carting coal all night. It was round-the-clock kind of work in those days.
And then about half past five that night, teeming with rain, bang bang on the door—open the door, and these two shivering guys standing there.
'Ma'am, can we hire a room? It's mighty cold out here.'
They were drenching wet, and I said, 'No, we don't hire no rooms. You take you coat off and hang it on the line there.'
I said, 'You can come in here by the fire and get warm.'

    And they were donned with cans of beer and all sorts of drink, and meat, and steak and goodness knows what-have-you.
They come inside, 'Can we use your cooker?', you know, to cook their food.
I said, 'Oh, help yourself'—showed them the kitchen.

US troops marching to camp, Paekakariki, 1942.
Alexander Turnbull Library

Next minute there was about thirty more of them arrive—I didn't see, there was a gang of them behind my hedge! I ended up with 32 of them. Yeah, and they were all cold and shivering.

However, they're cooking and everything else, and they had their own chewing gum and peanuts, cans of drink, things like that—they were giving it to my kids. And one came over to me and said, 'Would you like some pogey bait?'
I said, 'What's that?'
'Chocolate.' Oh yes. And they had loads of chocolate, you know, American chocolate and what not.

And so they made themselves comfortable.
One guy had a guitar, so I got them to get the kids to sing—my kids knew how to sing Maori songs.
And they said, 'What do you call you people?'
I said, 'Oh, we're Maoris. We're the native of New Zealand.'
'What's that?' says one fella.
'Well didn't you go to school? Didn't you know about New Zealand? We're Kiwis.'
'Aw. Do you have slimey limeys here?'
I said, 'What's that?'
They said, 'Poms.'
Because we'd never heard of that. 'Slimey limeys' they called Pakehas. I never knew about that.

So I said to them, 'Well, what state are you from?'
And one of them looked at me. 'Do you know about America?'

I said, 'Oh yes. We had Mormon Elders come here from Utah since 1928.'
Oh, that was quite a shock . . .

Anyway, I said to them, 'Do your parents know where you are?'
They said no.
'Well, you give me your addresses. They'll know next week where you are.'
'How come?'
'I'll write to them.'
They were struck quite dumb again.

Well I did that, I wrote to several of them—back came the letters.
So the parents knew that their kids were here in New Zealand. I just put, 'I guess you'd be thinking where Jed . . . (or so-and-so, whoever it was) . . . wondering what they're doing today. They're okay, they're climbing the hills at the moment, and been out swimming, or down here having Sunday dinner.' And I'd say, 'Colin went with us to a 21st birthday party last night.'
And they'd write back and say, 'What's that—21st?' And you write 'coming of age'. Because they don't have those sort of things.
So my correspondence with them in actual fact started right from day one. And I kept writing to the Yank families. I'm still writing . . . right till now . . . unless they die and I've got nobody to write to, but I still do, yeah.

Anyway, our house was full of people that night. My husband came home, but he arrived with officers. I only had these little PFCs—what they call, Private First Class—and a couple of sergeants. But he arrived with a blimmin colonel and a major, and some other baboon like that, who came in and looked the guys up and down and said, 'What . . . no tie . . . not right!' and all this, and ordering them back to the camp.
'No you don't,' I said, 'this is my house. They were here first, and if anybody's going to go it's going to be you, don't think because you've got the pips up there you're going to tell people what to do in my house.'
Yeah. I was just a total big mouth. Wouldn't let them kick the kids out—just because their ties weren't straight and la, la, la. Oh, I tell you they were fussy.

First day in they bought all our shops out of food, because their rations hadn't arrived yet. And so the pub was dry, by nine o'clock that night. They drank like fish.
Some were a bit scared of them because they were told that they were criminals—from out of prisons—they were the scruffy lot of America that were coming. They weren't really . . . no more than I was . . . it's just what our people thought. Some of them were only babies—17-, 18- and 19-year-olds. They were like ours, part of us. We got to know some really well.
Oh, shucks yes . . . in fact I was going to show you a picture of Horace in his dress uniform. He was only 16 and a half, this

kid. Yeah! He was down for 18 though. He got killed
on Tarawa.

Little tutai! Little brats. I used to tell lies for them.
There'd be skirts coming out from town or from up north or
wherever, some of them used to go AWOL and expect me to tell
the Commanding Officer a lie for them. I'd say, 'Only once.
Next time you can paddle your own canoe.'
I used to have old Colonel Jeske around my little finger
because I was doing his laundry and if he set up rough with
the boys I liked, 'Then do you own laundry,' I used to say.
    People didn't know what characters the guys were. They
thought they were a pack of criminals from out of prisons
over in the States. It was the first impression everybody got.
I had three coppers going this particular day, outside on the
lawn—boiling, because they were very fussy about their
clothes—their undies and whatnot—they had to be totally
boiled and ironed, some starched and so on. Wellington and
the Hutt couldn't cope with all the Yanks' drycleaning so the
local people were doing all this.
Anyhow, this particular day, these guys came and they turned
my hose on, into each of the coppers that I had fired up to
boil, and of course all the ashes and everything ended up in
amongst all the boiling clothes and what have you.
So I go out there—and they're standing there laughing. 'I'll
make you laugh,' I said and ran down the village and got one
of the MPs—grabbed these guys, didn't know them from Adam,

but said, 'Righto, go up and see what these guys have done.'
Well they arrested two of them, the others took to the scrapers. However they all got picked up for saying to me, 'Black, black, black,' and all this sort of tommyrot.
I said, 'You're not in America now and anyhow the black's as good as you. They might be black on the outside, but they're white at heart.'
The Maori put up a pretty good battle, eh. Yeah. I said to them, 'Don't talk like that, you're in Kiwi-land now. We don't have that sort of language here. So, look out!'

They got arrested anyway, and they had to pay—I got a big cheque for it. The Commanding Officer came and apologised and everything. But a lot of them used to be . . . mostly from New York. Smarties. Some bad ones kicked up bobsy-die. Mostly, they were alright.

But them that were home in the village . . . they used to lock their daughters up at seven o'clock at night. No outsies for them. And then we had lots of people come into work in the milk bars that were built overnight, so I accommodated the Maori parts of it.
Well they got engaged to endless marines, these Maori girls. Getting engaged every other day to different marines. The guys were buying diamond rings and what-have-you. Bouquets of flowers, and all sorts of things like that. They were very generous. They were well paid of course.
I said, 'That's just overnight sort of thing—guys can go and get killed, you don't want to do them for their money, spending it

on diamond rings and things like that.'

    I'll tell you what, the third night the guys were in here, in Paekakariki, there were women . . . from Wellington . . . oh, they were like blowflies . . . they used to come in carloads. Must have been 60 or 70—coming out here looking young lambs and they're old hoggets! All done up and painted and whatnot! Anything from 18- to 80-year-olds and *old ladies* with these guys.

    And Colonel Jeske—he ended up having my mother's house—when they pulled down the old homestead, they built this cottage out on the waterfront. And Colonel Jeske saw my mother and rented it to entertain his lady friends.
Anyhow, one night he invited three out at the same time, they all landed on the doorstep, so he was very unpopular, eh? So he immediately gave the key to me and said, 'Tell your Mum I don't need it anymore. I've got a cottage in Wellington.' Yeah.

Practically all through the war we had endless earthquakes . . . the biggest hazard we had during the war actually. Bringing up kids was alright, but the earthquakes—night and day—which was strange . . . and I'd hear all this screaming going on down the bank and I'd rush out to see what's wrong because everything's totally blackout—total blackout and you've got these women screaming . . . uhuh . . . someone's getting done over down there, I'll go and have a look.
My husband used to say, 'Don't ever go out that door. You don't know who's out there.' And he used to talk about rape . . . well,

you didn't even think of rape in those days . . .
but me, I'm nosy and I went to have a look—the old surf-club shed on the beach—a stilty thing, collapsed in a heap and it had about ten marines and ten women in there, anything from 18 to 80, old ladies with these guys . . . crack up . . . christ, the jolly thing collapsed!

    I used to do a stroll along the waterfront parade in Paekakariki—a lot of them used to come down to the guys and sleep on the beach with them . . . I used to go along with a blimmin stick and if I saw any Maoris I'd give them a whang. Tell them to get back to where they come from, whoever they were, or whatever they were. Yeah.

    Too right. They only there for the dollars . . . I was a fair old bag as far as that was . . . mind you I was 31, with two children of my own.

Did any of them ever try it on with you?

Heck no . . . soon show them around the corner.
    But most of the girls, soon as they finish work at the refreshment rooms, the train used to take them back to their digs, drop them off and pick them up and bring them back on duty at the refreshment rooms in the morning. And I says to their boss, I said, 'You know that train's not going to run very long, because those girls will be with those guys before you know where you are.'
And it happened. Train only ran for four nights.

We hardly slept. Everybody had to do war jobs, it didn't matter who you were . . . irrespective of having kids or whatever. See, we were busy, apart from the Yanks being here, we were also doing preserving puha and tahu-ing pauas and mussels and that to send to our Battalion boys over there, as well as the usual family chores. That was okay, because my sister Noeline was pregnant, so she had my girls, Yvonne and Monica. We had it all sussed out. I used to have to clean the Liberty trains, hop on the last one, finish that at 3 in the morning and start this laundry business straight away.

I used to have to take care of three trains—they were called Liberty trains, for the boys to go on leave from McKay's Crossing to Wellington Railway Station . . . they used to load up at the crossing to go into town. And it was quite an exciting job because . . . you'd go to clean them in the morning, you'd end up with a bucketful or two buckets of billfolds, diamond rings, all sorts of things like that.

I suppose they were going to give it to their dolls the next night when they go into town again. Engagement rings, beautiful ones.

And you'd spend about an hour and a half just signing those things in. And their billfolds were all chock-a-block with dollars and that . . . So I'd take them into the office where they had an American guy there that was in charge of all their personal things. I'd just hand them over, sign up, sign in what you found. And then let your crew, or yourself, go and clean up the train, see that it was just so so. Inside and out.

You know, people said our people were killing them. But they were doing it themselves. They'd be running to catch a unit, they'd be as drunk as skunks, and instead of getting in the unit they'd get on top of it—lie there, on top of the roof. And of course by the time the train pulled out, they'd roll off the top, eh? Onto the track and get killed. Some of them used be killed in the Liberty train—stabbed and all that. They were mean to one another. We'd find them in the toilet . . . I never ever found them because I'd be the whitest Maori on earth if I ever found one in the toilet . . . but the girls used to find them like that. Or so near death it didn't make any difference.

One of my younger sisters was on the trams—clippy on the trams. They only worked shift work, and we had a violent Maori Welfare Officer in those days. She happened to be our grand-aunt who's 99 now, Kuini Te Tau, was the first Maori Welfare Officer in Wellington and she used to do the rounds, and god help you if she catched you in a movie or something like that. And Irene my younger sister, who, although I say it myself, was quite attractive, you know, she'd line up with a different marine all the time. Come off the tram in her uniform straight into a movie with a marine. And anyhow, the grand-aunt went creeping in there. Came half-time there's Irene sitting there like Jackie scoffing popcorn with a guy. And she just didn't go and say, 'Can I speak to you a minute?'—she dragged her out of the movies just like that! She just gave her the third degree.

Well my sister was very smart. She said, 'You've got a cheek to

do that to me. I'm going back in the movies.'
'No you're not, you're supposed to be doing a war job.'
And she wouldn't let her go back in the movie. They had to go to the tramway office and check out whether she had finished her day's work or not. She'd finished her shift. Oh yes, she's off duty.

You see, we in Paekakariki didn't have to come to Wellington for nothing. There was a big place for dancing and everything. We knew what was going on at the ANA Club, and Te Hokowhitu Maori Club, you name it—the Army Navy and the Air Force were supposed to be the la-di-da outfits—Pakeha run that. But we had our own entertainment out there. The three camps had these massive halls, and we had different shows coming in. Not just Maori acts, culture clubs and things like that, they had their own entertainment too. There was a different show every night. We used to have all the latest movies in Saint Peter's hall and they'd have a band playing outside the hall, playing nursery rhymes for the kids in the afternoon and jazzy stuff for us adults at night. So we had stacks of entertainment. It was really good. You wouldn't even think there was a war on.

    Oh boy did we used to dance! . . . we had to have these flared skirts, and I always made sure to go once a week in there because they had all this jiving music.
Oh, gosh . . . dance! . . . Maoris, although I say it myself, but

Dance for US soldiers at McKay's Crossing, 1943. US National Archives

Maoris got this thing about them eh? Timing. Music. Dancing.
And it didn't matter what dance.
We used to chase the Negros in particular—oh, we used to
chase after them because they could dance, *really dance*. They
were really good.
Used to have good fun.

    My husband used to come too. Unless he was tired and
he'd stay home with the kids and then Noeline and I'd go.
They used to think we were single girls. And we had more
Yanks than single girls had. But then they respected us,
because they knew us. I wouldn't go with anything.
My sister Irene and Norma, they went with these Yanks to
town to some show or other. Coming home well the Yanks
dropped it on them, you know, wanted to do their thing with
them. 'Oh no way,' says the Maoris.
'Oh well you can walk home.'
And they walked from Pukerua Bay back home to Paekak . . .
feet all worn . . . almost bleeding, eh?
And these guys would go past on their jeep and, 'Care for
a ride?'
And Norma said she felt like getting the heel of her shoe and
poking it in their eye. So that when a couple of good nice-guys
came along and offered them a ride—they were too
frightened—they'd learnt their lesson.
When they got home, feet sore . . . I said, 'Good job, that's what
you get for just picking up anything.'

Oh what a laugh. Part of experience.
But my sister got engaged to one of the guys, she got engaged to this major and he got killed on Tarawa.
Most of them went away and got killed. And what didn't get killed, came back from Tarawa and Guadalcanal with malaria . . . it was nothing to walk along down the street in Paekakariki picking them up. Some of them were lying there dead on the road. Yeah. Oh, it was really sad.

And there was tragedy of all tragedies. The American transport ships arrived between Mana and Kapiti with amphibian tanks on board to be unloaded onto the beach.
A dirty southerly came up that day and two or three of them collided and tipped over. There was a big hullabaloo here on shore because they shouldn't have never unloaded them — 103 of them got drowned. We were picking bodies up there for days . . . those were guys that didn't even get to the war . . . a terrific blimmin tragedy that was. We watched the tides and the bodies would come up ashore. We got 83 of them. We'd wrap them up and put them up on the bank so they wouldn't get washed back out into the sea again. Three days we were picking up bodies.
And for years after . . . in fact a guy at Paekakariki has just found a dog tag of one of the guys . . . just came up a month or so ago.

What with the Japs out there we could have been minced up

without the Yanks. We were glad to have them. The Japs certainly worried us alright.

This particular night we had a real big party, because Maoris weren't allowed to have beer in their homes then. That was the law then but the Yanks used to get it all, 'hogsheads' as we called them, 18 gallon kegs. Get two or three of them up on the truck and take it up to my Mum's house, and we used to party on up there.

And this particular night, there was a big rage on, and we were all drinking and singing and what-have-you. And we went outside to the toilet, and there was only one toilet, and it was one of these drop jobs, so . . . we couldn't all get in there at once so we were all stooping around in the lupins.

And we heard this weird noise. Now, you know, Maoris have a karanga and things like that eh, and in the still of the night it was quite weird. Well this sound started up. Queer. Really weird. I thought all our ancestors had come to life . . . it sounded *terrible*.

Half of us . . . didn't have time to pull up our tweeds . . . rushing inside screaming. The Yanks, my husband and all the Maori boys came rushing out to see what's wrong. And the blimmin Yanks cracked up laughing and said it was Navajo Indians. They had a Navajo Indian company based up the top of Paekakariki hill—the other part of the signal corps was in Paekakariki down in the camp itself.

'Oh we'd better get back to camp. There's something wrong.' And the siren went over in the camp so they all took off.

There was a Jap submarine out in the sea somewhere.

Lots of the boys have passed on. They were like ours; part of us.
Ours were over in the Middle East, our cousins and what-have-you. All young people. Like extended family . . . their wives . . . I've got two godchildren as well.
Sid Shapiro, brother Sidney, yeah. He was choice. He was one of Mum's 'babies'. She arranged special leave for Sid three times, he became engaged to a Maori girl in Rotorua, but on the last time he was away for a fortnight. That was when he was sent to Kapiti for punishment.
After the war he married and his wife was—what do you call it? . . . like Woolworths? Barbara-what's-it . . . Hutton? Sidney's wife belonged to a well-known family. They even had aeroplanes.
Esther and Sid used to do parcels up for the kids and Mum and all of us—Yvonne and Monica. Esther passed away and Sid was going to remarry again and he wrote to all of us girls—'Dear Sis,' he wrote to each of us—'I'm thinking about remarrying. So do you mind if I get married again?' And the three of us said, 'YES WE DO. We don't want you to get married again.' But he did.
And then he passed away suddenly, and his wife was quite choice, because she came out and she brought back the old lemon squeezer hat—actually it's in our museum at Paekakariki—and all the money and all the different things

Jean, second from left, 1948. Her sister, Irene, is on the left, and her mother, Miriona Budge, is second from the right

that Esther had left in their will for us and my kids. Choice. Really choice.

And when Mum died . . . and my sister called Sid up and told him. He wanted to come over to her funeral, but didn't make it.
But when we took Mum's body up to the cemetery, here was this *massive* wreath which covered the whole of the grave, and it was the marine emblem, red white and . . . massive big red white and blue ribbon on it, and it just covered the whole of her grave. Then he rang us that night to ask how many came to the funeral for 'Mom'. Mmmm . . .

I tell my mokopuna about the war years. We go up there to the cemetery and sit there and they say, 'What's that concrete slab down there in the motor camp?'
And I'll say 'Aw, that's where the 8th Marines were. That's where Uncle Sid's hut was,'
or something like that. Tell them all about it.
Sit up there for hours talking. Yeah. I've got nothing to do but that now. Talk to them.

When the Yanks left, it was dead silence. Back to norm. Back to about a population of 500 or so. Absolutely back to square one. Absolutely dead. Dead silence. Yeah.
The sound that I will ever remember though is those
Indians and their war cry at night. It was so weird. So out of the ordinary.

Some of Jean's family, 1950s. From left: sister Muri, Jean, Jean's mother Miriona Budge, sisters Irene and Heeni (front)

After the war, Auntie Jean raised three more children of her own and whangai/cared for many welfare children, right up until 1990. She was awarded the QSM (Queen's Service Medal) for her eighteen years of voluntary work for the Justice, Social Welfare and Probation Departments. For many, she was a welcome and familiar figure around the Courts.

She was a long-time member of the Maori Women's Welfare League, and deeply committed to, and involved with, Kohanga Reo. Over many years, she served time on all the local school committees, being a great believer in education. She was herself renowned as a teacher of kowhaiwhai.

The recognition she possibly valued the most was the acknowledgement given over the years by the American Marines, and their families, for her support for nearly 50 years. As members of the 6th, 8th and 10th Marines, units of the First and Second Divisions, made their regular pilgrimages back to the site of their camps (Russell, McKay's Crossing, Paekakariki, Paraparaumu and Pauahatanui) —'home' during the war— Auntie Jean was always on hand to make them welcome and help them relive their youthful memories. In 1968 she had the honour of being made a Life Member of the National Second Marine Division, and was awarded, for services rendered to the returning parties, the Golden Brooch, a special emblem presented only to the wives of marines.

'So I am one of the proud owners, and the only one I presume in New Zealand that's got one. I cherish it very much.'

Jean receiving the Queen's Service Medal, 1986. On left, her eldest child Yvonne; on right, her youngest child Karl. Joe Hughes, *Photo News,* Wainuiomata

Only two days after her interview was filmed, Auntie Jean was diagnosed as having lung cancer and within a matter of weeks she was dead. Her body now rests, along with her tipuna, up on the hill in the cemetery that she once physically defended. She bitterly and successfully opposed the Government who wanted to move the graves to the sand-dunes and use the land for other purposes.

Haere ra Auntie Jean.
Kia kaha.

Jean, standing in her commemorative rock garden at her Paekakariki home, to welcome former members of the US Marines Second Division, 1992. *Evening Post*

Florence Small

(née Macey, formerly Lassen)

*F*lo grew up in a lively family of seven in Newtown, a working class suburb of Wellington. She left school at 14 to work at Kirkcaldie and Stains department store, first mending nylon stockings and then behind the counter. She left that job to work as a scullery maid at Wellington Public Hospital, where she eventually became first cook. Before the war, Flo was a typical young woman, making the most of her youthful independence, leading an exuberant social life.

I was different from other girls. My mother always said, 'You should have been born in the next generation because they don't understand you.'
I think because I did things that people thought were wicked and I did them because I wanted to.

I wore a bathing costume that everybody thought was absolutely wicked. And it wasn't, it was practically neck-to-knee.
And I done things. I danced and enjoyed myself and laughed. I wore slicey hats with veils that I put little spots on and I wore dresses that my mother made and then I altered and made shorter when you shouldn't show your legs.
And I liked clothes that were very bright. Like in those days it was very wicked to wear red shoes and I *loved* red shoes and when I went to work I saved up and bought a pair of red shoes and I sneaked wearing them.

I hid my red shoes in the milk box when I went out—what we used to do was put a pair of black shoes on and mum used to put the shoes in the milk box for us and we used to take them off as we went out and put the red shoes on and when we came back we'd put the red shoes there and mum would come out and hide them. Mum hid them under the bed.

What did you feel like when you had those red shoes on?

Oh wonderful. Felt I was a hussy. Just a hussy. Absolutely a hussy!

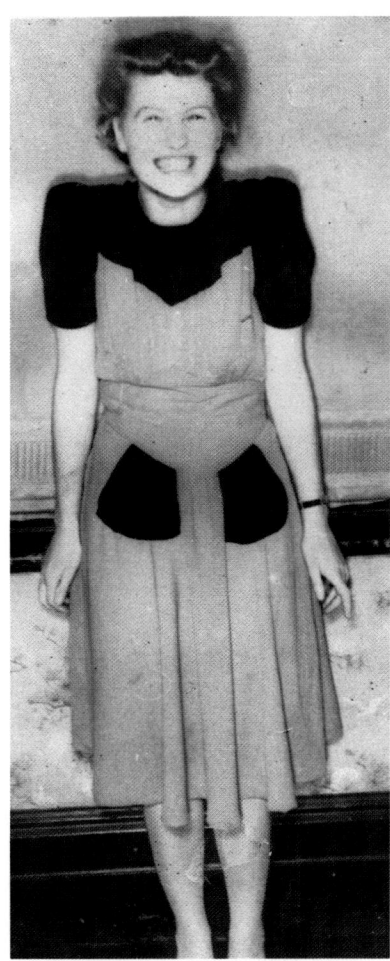

'I was always wicked'—Flo, 1939

And we used to spend all Saturday on a funny old sewing machine that mum had, Singer, funny old treadle, treadling away making these dance dresses, you know. You see, we didn't really go around in sack-cloth. We did make nice dresses, because we got our stuff from Evans which was a shilling a yard.

And another thing we did, which girls would laugh at these days, we swapped dresses. Like there was three of us. We used to have a long black taffeta skirt and I used to have a lamé top or a yellow one. Molly had a red one and Annie had another colour and then we'd go to the dance on Saturday night and then the following Saturday night we'd still have the black skirt on, but we'd swapped tops.

And I remember also, at the town hall once a year there used to be a ball and all us girls would go and mum made me a beautiful tulle dress. Tulle, and it had a white satin top, no sleeves and she made me this velvet coat to go with it. Short, velvet coat. Had big puffy sleeves and gathers and I bought this hunk of fur for a shilling. Hah! Honestly, we thought we were Christmas!

Mostly we danced with girls because there was a shortage of boys. We learned to dance with girls.

We used to have in our house a dining room, no carpet of course in those days, it was congoleum. And we had an old gramophone with a big green horn, His Master's Voice, and we played these records like 'If You Knew Susie' which was very daring—we loved it—the tunes were really funny when I think

Flo in a 'slicey hat with veil'

of it . . . 'You'll Be Pa I'll Be Mama.'
Very daring, very daring for those days, let me tell you.
    Well, it was how people were, in those days. People were, shall we say, narrow-minded?
But that's how our mothers were brought up. You can't kind of blame our generation. Our mothers never knew *anything*—they weren't told *anything*.
Sex was a wicked word. Love was a wicked word. It was whispered. Like years and years ago I can remember, we had a funny old sink and my mother standing and doing dishes and my father came along and pat mum on the bottom and she said, 'Don't do that John in front of the children.' We were 16 and 18! Now, can you imagine it, nowadays? You see it's a different generation isn't it?
But I thought it was lovely and I loved my father, kissing mum on the back of the neck, I thought that was cute.
Always wishing that someone would kiss *me* on the back of the neck!
    Really when I think of it, even mum didn't know much about sex and how a woman who's married doesn't know about sex I don't know but still they didn't in those days.
Sex wasn't talked about. Periods weren't talked about. It was really so, so awful when you think of it. Very, very ignorant and stupid.
You know where I thought babies came from? I thought babies came from either out of your stomach or out of your bottom. Absolutely stupid. I mean doesn't it make you sick now?

And I remember sneaking a Marie Stopes book, none of you would remember, but she wrote on sex, and reading this book bit by bit and couldn't make out what it was. I was reading this book when I was single, when it was wicked to read it. It was a hidden book and one of those books that came in brown paper when you sent away for it.

    But women have had sex, since the beginning of time, really. I mean if you go with a boy long enough sex is bound to come into it somewhere along the line and I'm not saying there are lots and lots of girls that did have sex—some didn't have sex before they were married—but I really think some of them did.

Did you?

No I didn't because—you know why?
I was dead scared of my father.
Yes. And that's the only thing that saved me because our father said if any of us 'got into trouble' as we called it in those days he'd murder us and I quite believe he would have. But there were times when I was tempted if I were truthful. Myself, I would never consider an abortion but they were easy to get. Very easy.
That's another thing . . . they think us old girls don't know anything . . . I remember we used to go work in the trams. And there used to be lots of little houses down Adelaide Road and you wouldn't know, but whispers go around. 'See that

house, a woman does abortions there. Twenty-five pounds.'
This is true, I can remember people saying this.
Everybody knows all these things—they just *say* they don't. I always used to look at these houses and think, ooh I wonder who's having an abortion, you know? Just wonder. And, in those days also, don't forget, lots of families weren't as kind. As soon as the girls were pregnant they kicked them out.

Actually, I actually saw this abortion.
I went there when a woman had it done somewhere in Miramar, I don't know where because I couldn't remember now anyway, don't forget it's 50-odd years or more. And she done her with the knitting needle and that was the first abortion that I ever seen. And the last I hope.
It was a terrible one. Absolutely terrible and the only thing that saved her was . . .
it doesn't matter now, mum's dead . . . I went home and told mum about all this blood that was in this house and my mother put her hat and coat on and went and got a midwife friend of hers and the midwife went down and looked after this girl. She would have died, I'm quite sure, if she hadn't. And my mother said, 'You don't say a word to *anybody* about this. Nothing. *Never* say a word.'
But everybody's dead now, it doesn't matter.

I will say that my friend said she was spotlessly clean. I can remember her saying that she wasn't charged the 25 pound and that she was spotlessly clean. I don't know if this is the right figure, but people reckon there were about twenty abortions a week during war time. I couldn't tell you whether that's true.

She used a knitting needle?

She used a knitting needle.

She couldn't have been very professional . . .

No, but lots of people, lots of wives tried themselves in those days with knitting needles.

When war broke out, I remember I had the flu, I was very ill with the flu, in bed and mother had made me beef tea. You never hear of beef tea now and she come along with this beef tea and she was crying, 'Aw. You know what's happened Florence?'
I thought the house had fallen in.
And she said, 'War's been declared.'
But I was quite callous I'm sorry. 'War declared', it didn't mean anything when you're young and it's amazing as war went on, we never thought, or I never thought, and I'm sure lots of young women like me never thought, anyone was going to die or get killed in war. That's how absolutely stupid it was. We didn't have the brains of a louse.
And even when lots of our boys had all got into uniforms and we gave farewell parties to them, we never thought for one

moment that any of them were going to get killed. Isn't it amazing that we could be so dumb?

    The reality struck our own family when *our* boys went to war.
They were thrilled to bits. I suppose it's just the same every war, they really think it's adventure, don't they? Men are different from women. I don't know whether it's a duty, but they all go and they were quite happy and I'm quite sure my brothers never thought they'd get killed.

But they were.

Yes, both them.

Within a month of one another.

John was first, to go
and we went down to the wharf where there were hundreds and hundreds—oh hundreds of people saying farewell and I don't think anybody wasn't crying because everybody on the wharf had suddenly realised that this *was* a war—
before it was kind of a fairy story—they were out at Trentham in camps and . . . they were still at home and they were still *your* boys and suddenly your boys were away on a big ship. We were waving madly. All those boys on the ship.
I remember my mother saying, 'How many of them will come back?' never thinking that ours wouldn't come back, because

every mother there thought her boy was coming back.
And it was depressing.

    We watched the ship go out and when we came home it
was depressing—there was nothing you can say, it's a kind of
funny . . . you cry and you go into a bedroom where
someone's been and you think of something that perhaps you
and your brothers have said, something funny,
and all of a sudden you don't really know what to do.
Now my mother scrubbed a bench and she scrubbed it about
four times. I remember mum with a scrubbing brush and a
cake of Electric sandsoap scrubbing this bench and I said,
'Mother, you've scrubbed that bench. What are you doing?'
She said, 'If I don't scrub it I'll go mad.'

    And my mother was quite religious. Mum prayed. I wasn't
a bit religious I'm sorry to say.
And I remember, we had a funny old seat down the garden
and when she got news of the boys being dead that's when her
and dad were down the garden holding hands and crying on
the seat. This funny old seat.
And what do you say to a mother and father that have lost
their sons?

    It was in the morning, actually. And in those days they
sent out little notices, to kind of like, let you know.
But, that's another thing, our boys had been dead . . . you
didn't [know], the day they died, you didn't get a notice. So
that everybody's sons were probably dead weeks, and mothers

Flo's mother and father, c.1949

were still sending, like my mother did, parcels to them
and things.
And, really I thought that day was the saddest in mum's life,
and dad's and our's.
But not only was it sad for us that day because four or five of
people that we knew in Newtown had lost sons too.
Women are wonderful, you know, of that generation. Getting
up and going to visit a neighbour who had lost her boy. Mum
had lost hers.
'I must go and see Mrs Miller, I must go and see her, she's lost
her boy.'
And my mother got dressed and went over and they probably
cried together.
    Because I was young and stupid I coped better than
mother. I don't care what you say, you don't think of death
when you're young and you just think well the boys are dead,
they're dead. But the thing that worried me was—and I
thought of it often—I never kissed them goodbye. We never put
flowers on a grave. I thought, there's nobody to put flowers on
their grave, which to me was dreadful.

My father's a funny old thing. Really he was. He was one-eyed
about girls going with boys and things . . .
Well it was a Saturday and, my father used to go fishing on the
wharf and he met these two Americans
that was Warren and Bill.

Mum had cut him a lunch and most unusual for my father, he shared it! Shared it with two *Americans*, which was really funny. It made mum and I laugh when we found out. And he invited these two boys back for tea.
Now in those days, people were very prejudiced against Americans and we had a very nosy neighbour and I mean nosy. And, my father walks in with two Americans in uniform.
You can imagine what it was like, in a small street. And my mother's at the sink and she said to me, 'I'll bet Mrs Thompson's looking through that curtain.' And mum and I rush up to the bedroom and we pull the bedroom curtain across and sure enough there's Mrs Thompson glaring out. Hah! Mum and I roared, roared and thought it was very funny. And of course she couldn't wait . . . a few days after, she came over to Mum and she said, 'Is Florence going with an American? I saw John bring two Americans to your place Mabel. That's not very patriotic because you know what the Americans are.'
That's what she said to my mother. And my mother told her off and my mother was a gentle woman. My mother said, 'If you spent more time at the back instead of at the curtain worrying about my daughter,' she said, 'it would be better.'
I remember mum saying that.
    But anyway, they came for tea.
Well in those days there was no fridges and when mum cooked, she just cooked enough and here we were scrimping

on things and mum whispering to dad, 'I wish you had let me know John. I could have got something else in.'

But they were very nice, Warren and Bill. They made the best of everything. 'Aw, don't worry,' that's why we liked them probably, and sat at our funny old table, because don't forget we had no money in those days. Poor as church mice really when I look back.

And they sat at the table and they made it seem as though it was a lovely meal. We played cards a lot—500 and Euchre—and we all played that night and it was real nice, and I kept looking at Warren and thinking how nice he was really, you know. And I thought, 'Oh Lord if I make a date with him there'll be trouble,' I could see dad, you know?

But anyway, all out of the blue dad said, 'Now every leave, you boys are to come up here.'

Mum and I nearly dropped dead through the floor. We thought, good Lord this is a change of heart! We couldn't believe that he'd say that.

Anyway we just started going out and going out, and that's how it started.

I thought Warren was so nice and he did things for me and he treated me nice and I liked it.

I kind of got to . . . it was more than *like*, you know?

And we went to a wedding of a friend of his who'd married a New Zealand girl and we were at the wedding and I said, 'Isn't it a lovely wedding Warren? Isn't it lovely? I'm so glad they're so happy.'

And he just said, 'It should be us, shouldn't it?'
And that's how it was. We got engaged. Then we got married. And ooooh yes! Everybody waited for me to get pregnant. They all thought I was pregnant of course, *before* we got married. Ha. Ha.

Would you like to know when we got married? Right. Well it was very funny because in those days everything was rationed you know and we had a very nice breadmaker in Newtown who knew mother, who made a cake—it was all 'under the table'—currants and sultanas and things, sandwiches. The butcher gave us ham and lovely stuff. We paid for it like, you know mum had paid for it, but it was kind of . . . didn't fall off a lorry like, but it kind of was sneaky. Sneaky's the word. Even the clothes I wore were sneak . . . you had to have coupons to get things, and Regent Gowns were very good to me, they saw that I got nice clothes and my bridesmaid got things.
And everything went nice.
We had jellies and stuff like that and flowers.
I had lovely aunts. Wonderful aunts. They thought we were marvellous—they were kind of all on our side. If I were to have committed ten murders, that would have been alright you see because I belonged to the family. It's a strange thing about families, but there is a tie there, even in this generation. And they all picked flowers from their garden and made a lovely spray, marvellous, and flowers all round the room. Everything was lovely.

Flo's official engagement photograph. Willis Street Studio, Wellington

Everybody thought I was pregnant—I bet everybody counted—and I'm sorry to tell you I wasn't. But when I did get pregnant I was quite amazed to tell you the honest truth because I was a bit dumb about that really.

Warren rushes home, and don't forget we're young, and all we do is rush into bed and I remember saying, 'If I get pregnant will you be sad or happy?'

And he said, 'Happy' and never thought any more about it. And then when we went to a little place down in Courtenay Place and had a meal and all through the meal I got the giggles because people didn't rush to bed I suppose. Only me. And I thought this is funny and all these people and us having meals and we'd just got out of bed you see and that bit tickled my fancy.

And he kept saying to me, 'What are you laughing at?' and I said, 'You know what I'm laughing at?' I said, 'I wonder if all these people that are sitting here, eating all this steak and stuff, knew that we'd just got out of bed!' and he said, 'Well do I get up and tell them you're pregnant or not?'

I always remember this, it was really funny.

And, then, don't laugh, I *was* pregnant! And that made me laugh because it was a rush job. I thought, you don't really get pregnant until you kind of have a few weeks and things, you know. Not just one rush job, but one rush job did it!

I wrote to Warren, I wrote every day actually, and told him I was pregnant which he was thrilled to bits with and he wrote back—he'd been transferred onto another warship—not only

Warren's official engagement photograph. Willis Street Studio, Wellington

him, I suppose there were 20 or 30 of them got transferred to the warship and then, you see the Jap torpedo got them. Warren was killed.
I never thought that the ship would get torpedoed. I thought he was safer on a ship. And Warren wasn't like the average American. People say oh the Americans were terrible, they buy you flowers and roses and stuff like that. But don't forget he was 36 and all he wanted was . . .
Warren didn't want to go to war but unfortunately he was in the navy permanent when war broke out and that's what happened. And the saddest thing for me was thinking he's never going to see Steph.
The saddest day . . . it was dreadful . . . he only wanted a child and a house and a wife and he's got all that and he's not here . . . and I couldn't cope. I couldn't believe it.
I wasn't, I'm sorry I wasn't interested in all the other boys that got killed, the New Zealanders, because I didn't go with them I went with Warren.
That was my main day, where I really couldn't cope.
And my mother loved Warren and I felt it was terrible for mum to have the boys killed and then Warren.

    Well it was absolutely a terrible day. Do you know, when your husband or lover or someone that you love dies, it's funny all the things that run through your mind? I couldn't really believe it. That it could happen to me. I thought that I was the only person in New Zealand that this had happened to. I thought I'd never be able to cope. I thought I'm

pregnant—but a funny thing, although I was pregnant I never thought of abortion. All I thought of was that I must have this baby, I must get well because another thing in our day, pregnancy, it was kind of a life-and-death thing.
I used to say to mum pray for me that if I die someone will look after the baby because I thought wouldn't it be terrible if Warren and I were both dead and this baby was amongst this world. And I *hated* the world. I'm sorry, I did. I hated it. I thought that of all the people in it, only my family and my aunts and uncles and couple of very good friends who had been very kind to me, were worth even thinking about. I thought the rest of the world was wicked. I thought there's not a Christian attitude in it and that's what I thought on that day. And another thing, I know someone, a girl who I grew up with, who went with an American who got killed who slit her two wrists. But I never thought of doing that either.

I was working at Kirkcaldies and Stains and I had to leave as soon as I got a bit big of course, because in those days when you're pregnant nobody worked and then trouble started because I had no money. There I was having a baby.
I went into this lovely wee private home that used to be in Willis Street, it's not there now. But anyway I went two days and two nights in labour and the nurses were absolutely wonderful to me. Those nurses knew Warren was dead and that, I kind of got crying, whether with pain and worrying and having a baby. Not a bit brave. I know a lot of women say they're brave, I wasn't brave. Nothing brave about having a

baby, it's awful. And anyway they were really nice. They were kind and when Stephanie was born, they made lots of fusses of me—you see there's some people never thought about people being married to an American—they'd bring me little bunches of violets, a little cake, they were wonderful those nurses, to me, and the old doctor—can't even remember who he was. He was nice.
'You're my favourite patient,' he said, 'and this is my favourite baby.'
I said, 'You don't mean it.'
'Yes I do,' he said. 'You're a strong lady.'
And I always remember him saying that.
Now that I look back I think how did I ever think I was going to get through it? No money, a poor family and too proud probably to write to Warren's mother and father and say would they help us. I don't know how I managed it. I don't really. And I don't know how I got over, over that death because everybody was so, nasty and sniggery, and didn't care a tuppenny. I heard someone saying, 'Americans' . . . actually saying about the American Indians when they were killed . . . 'aw, it didn't matter because they were a Red Indian.' And that was the attitude that people had with Americans.
It didn't matter how many mothers were over there crying just like our mothers, it didn't matter that they got killed.
It was a terrible attitude for people who are supposed to be a loving kind race of people.
Neighbours and people that my mother knew said things,

horrible things. 'Oh, I suppose she'll pick with one of our soldiers now and marry them so they'll keep the American's kid.' Things like that.
They'd have put me on a stake and lit a fire under me, I'm sure. Listen, don't forget, there were a lot of nice girls had babies.

But I'll tell you something funny about prejudice. How people are. Warren was American but had German blood in him. Now when my father, after we'd been married and I was going to have Stephanie, my father was very nasty to me about Warren because he had German blood in him and yet, like it's a grandfather . . . goes back. Like mine's Irish. Irish as Paddy's pigs. You know what I mean? And yet he was so prejudiced, he was so one-eyed English, really because we were fighting Germans—the Germans that Warren was fighting just the same as anyone else.

Did this create problems then, between you and your father?

It created terrible problems, that's why I moved into a bedsit and went to work scrubbing floors. And I took Stephanie down to the Catholics at the Basin Reserve and they minded her. The nuns were lovely to me—they were really kind for me and understood and never said anything.
This went on for ages and I wasn't managing. I had been trying to get money from the American Ambassador . . . Warren and I were married when you didn't have to get a

certificate, then the Americans brought out a rule that
Americans marrying New Zealand girls had to get permission.
Well because we never had permission, I couldn't get a
pension and I couldn't get a pension from New Zealand
authorities even though Warren was fighting for all of us,
couldn't get a pension from there because he wasn't a
New Zealander.
And so it was very, very difficult
and then I went home because my mother insisted because
she saw me getting probably thinner and Stephanie and
everything to look after because things were very bad and
people were very cruel to me when I had Stephanie.
As a matter of fact, when Stephanie was in a pram once, one
lady came and looked at her. Lifted the little cover up and
said, 'You know, I thought she'd be black.'
'Why?' She said because all Americans have got nigger blood
in them.
    And I had to put up with all that
and then I had a girlfriend and because I had married an
American her mother wouldn't let us be friends. As a matter
of fact I went to school with her, we grew up together and we
were always friends through everything. And she was just the
same, 'They're all niggers.'
Anyway my girlfriend said to me, 'Oh Flo,' she said, 'I can't let
you come home any more.'
And I said, 'Why?'
She said, 'Because mum says she doesn't want our boys to get

on with you or you to get on with the boys because you've got the American's baby.'
And I was that hurt. Anyway I said to the mother, 'I'm very sorry,' I said, 'I have no intention of getting on with your boys. Ever,' and I left.
And all the way home I cried and when I got home I told mum and she put her arms around me and she said never mind. My mother never swore. She said, 'It doesn't matter a *damn*, we love Stephanie and we love you. And that's all in this world that matters.'

So was this a scandalous thing that you're married to an American?

Oh it was terrible. It was like me being a prostitute, I was like, the most wickedest woman in New Zealand. And that's how it was. Absolutely terrible.
Even neighbours in our street who had been friends with my mother kind of snubbed me and snubbed mum. I think it was because a lot of girls gave up New Zealand soldiers for Americans. That's all I can think of.
But you're not going to tell me that all our New Zealand forces went overseas to Italy, England all these places and Scotland, everywhere. Didn't marry, fall in love, or have affairs with girls, overseas. That's amazing. You're making out that our, all the boys were absolutely saints?
I can't believe that. I can't believe it. They married English

girls, Scottish girls. Probably some of them married French girls, German girls, and yet nobody said that they were men with two heads.

I mean, I wasn't a young stupid girl. I knew what I was doing. I was 26 by then, and I knew what I was doing and I mean nobody else wanted me. Let's look at that. I didn't have another boyfriend so it wasn't as though I was breaking hearts, was it?

It made me bitter. It did. Actually I could have spat in their eye, if I can say that. I really could. I could have. Because, I thought, Warren gave you his life. He died fighting for a cause that wasn't even his.

There was nobody to talk to. I just cried. I really made myself real miserable, really.

And sometimes when I was real miserable, I used to take Stephanie and walk right up by the fire brigade station and I'd go and just sit on the benches at Evans Bay with her, and think. I'd sit there for a long while and a thought might come into my head, like, 'Well I've got Stephanie, I'm alive. I've got a life before, I'll just have to start again.'

And then I'd come home and feel much better and I'd say to mother, 'I've been sitting thinking. I'm not going to feel sorry for myself any more. I don't care a tuppenny damn what people think. I'm going to start my life and look after Stephanie and make another life.'

And that's what I did.

It didn't worry me that the war was over—war meant

Flo and Stephanie, c.1950

nothing to me then. It just became a thing, like you had three meals a day. I had no interest in war because everyone said we were going to win in any case.
But I thought the cost was too great.
The war changed our family. Somehow it changed from a nice happy family to a kind of remorseful family. There wasn't the happiness. There wasn't the laughter. There wasn't the birthday parties. When we, the family, all got together, uncles and aunts and everybody, there were too many cousins missing. Too many friends missing.
I'm not saying they were bitter, that would be wicked to say that, but I think deep down they were envious of people who were lucky enough to have sons and fathers, someone back.
I would be a liar if I didn't say I wasn't envious of other women and their husbands.
When the war had finished I was sad and most ungrateful, I suppose because I was left alone and I thought everybody came back happy.

As you know, I married again and I married a very nice man who was very understanding, who has treated Stephanie just like his own. Now, the feeling I had for Jim is different from the feeling that I had for Warren. And I can't explain that. He's been good to me and I have a wonderful daughter to him. Wonderful. I have two wonderful daughters, so I have been a very fortunate woman.
If I put my thoughts and things, or whatever they say, and

Stephanie (right) with her cousin Avis, 1949.
Elmar Studios, Palmerston North

weigh them up, I think that I've had a wonderful life.
I'm 80 and I've experienced, love, sex, everything that you can think of. Sorrow, poverty, but most of all, I have experienced a wonderful love from two men and two wonderful daughters. Which pleases me every day.

Despite being treated as an outcast, and the desolation of being a war widow, Flo, now in her eighties, has a gaiety and zest for life that invariably raises the spirits of those that come into contact with her.

For the past 13 years Flo has been involved in voluntary work for church charities, but not, she is quick to explain, because she is religious. 'Not a bit. I don't see eye-to-eye with what they see. But I like what they try to do.' Her care and concern for those down on their luck is directly related, she says, to the fact that the nuns were kind and accepting when she was a solo mother in a difficult situation.

Flo believes that war taught her to stand up for herself and to have faith in her ability to cope. She thinks she would be a different person today if she hadn't been through the war experience. 'I think it's taught me to be kinder, and I wouldn't have understood all what I understand now.'

Flo's mother used to say, 'Buy flowers for me now. Don't buy them when I'm dead' – it pleases Flo greatly that her own two daughters send her flowers every week.

Alister Doyle
(née Street)

Ali had just left school when war was declared. For her it was the end of family life as she had known it. A brother was already in the merchant marine and 'he just kept sailing, and I was the next one to go'. She had wanted to be a doctor, but knew that was impossible, so settled on being a nurse. Initially she was rejected because of her lack of height and because she wasn't considered strong enough. Ironically she ended up in an engineering factory working with heavy equipment designed for men to operate, making bombs during wartime. This gives her considerable pride and satisfaction today. She left nursing on the West Coast for a variety of jobs in Wellington including waitressing in tea rooms and milkbars, at the time the city was invaded by American marines.

The day that war was declared I was celebrating an 18th birthday and there we were in mum's dining room, half a dozen school friends, and we were waiting for news from Neville Chamberlain. It was 11 o'clock at night and we put on the radio to listen to Chamberlain say, 'We are now at war with Germany.' Of course that was the end of my birthday party.

Mother burst into tears and we all looked at one another. Most of us knew our school days were over, very soon we'd be into uniform here there and everywhere. It was this great big question mark hanging over all of us.

We never met as the family again. That was it.

September 1939 I left being a schoolgirl to be an adult. I put on a uniform and actually I lost those fun years that children have today, dining and wining and dancing, we didn't have any of it. We just went from one uniform to another within a few months and I had six years in some sort of uniform. I went nursing.

I had always wanted to be a doctor but those days girls were not pushed in education and in a large family, the girls didn't get to university unless the family were really rich and I mean *rich*.

Soon as war was declared I started looking to be a nurse, going to the hospitals to see if there was any vacancies. My first trial was Nelson hospital where the matron said, 'No, you're far too small, too tiny, not strong enough and you wouldn't last the distance.'

So I took this as an acceptance that I may not be getting into nursing but I wasn't ready to give up. So I came back home over the Christmas, went to Greymouth hospital and had the same procedure; Matron said, 'No, you're too small, not heavy enough. You couldn't last the distance.'

Nurse Alister Doyle

But I was determined to keep on trying.

Within a few days my sister-in-law had written from Westport to say there was a vacancy at Buller Hospital. So I sent a letter away and within days I received an acceptance . . . yes I was going to be a member of the staff and would I please bring black stockings, black shoes and a watch to take temperatures, and enclosed were the Public Service papers.

So I had to take these over to the family doctor to get them filled out correctly. He looked at me. 'No. I can't sign these papers, you're too small, you've been too ill, you're not heavy enough, you won't last the distance.' 'Well I'm not going to give up, I am going to keep on trying and if you don't fill my papers in I'll find someone who will.'

He had known me from way back. He said, 'Oh well, if that's the mood you're in I'll tell a few white lies for you.'

So he made my weight a little heavier, made my height a little taller and I scraped through by the skin of my teeth.

And in a few weeks time I was inducted into nursing at Buller Hospital, 7th of February 1940, measured up for uniforms, straight into the ward, without any pre-education whatsoever. They were so terribly short of staff with the senior nurses going into uniform to go overseas. Promotion was very quick. Nursing was hard—it was just like the army; if a senior nurse was two days your superior, she was boss—that was that—and if she said the moon was made of green cheese, that was it—you stood to attention, with hands behind your back and said, 'Yes nurse, the moon is made of green cheese.'

Ali during nurse training, Buller Hospital, 1941.
(Ali is in the front row, wearing a cardigan)

There was no argument. It was hard, hard work and you needed a sense of humour otherwise you give up after the first week. I sort of had a detached scientific approach to the work.

The most important person in the hospital is the patient and the first thing you do is to respect the patient's privacy and their secret life, otherwise they don't come for treatment. I was approached in the corridor one day by a local constable who wanted to know if there was anyone in the ward who'd had a self-induced abortion. He must have thought I was very simple-minded, 'cos I just looked him up and down and said, 'You don't expect me to tell you if there were do you?'

It wasn't the single girls—they did get into trouble but they went towards church people to support them if their parents didn't. It was the married women who had the abortions. When I was on duty it was always classically about nine or ten at night—some lady had 'fallen' down the back steps carrying a load of wood. It was no such thing of course, the reports came back from the theatre, it was quite different.
I suppose they were attacking themselves with needles or sharp objects; whatever was available at the time. There were back-garden abortionists but they kept their identities very secret because if they were caught they were punished and unfortunately the poor woman, if she was caught, she was punished too. It was illegal.

Somewhere along my middle years a patient was admitted and she was in her 30s and a Roman Catholic. There was this very strong religious feeling within the hospital, Protestant

versus Catholic, which was sad in a way. There was a division.
(The coast is very Irish in lots of ways, so you learn to live
with it. I was Protestant but quite a few of them were Catholic
and we all mixed together, we were all good girls.)

This lady was admitted this particular day, I was on night duty
at the time, she was found on the side of the road in a very
distressed physical condition. She was diagnosed as a
septicaemia following childbirth. The baby was dead and
had been for some time and it came away in pieces. She was
very ill.

This was in the days before antibiotics, we didn't have
penicillin or sulphanilamide and she was so infectious she
had to be nursed in isolation. She took a long time to die
slowly of septicaemia without once complaining or telling her
folks who was responsible. She was asked every day, by her
family, if she would take Confession. She didn't.

It was a very sad case—there it was, a wasted life, a wasted
child just because it wasn't proper for a single girl to be
unmarried with a child.

I don't know quite where to start, but I left nursing because of
ill health and family problems and romantic problems and
came to Wellington to marry a seaman. He was away at sea
and I was left to find my place in Wellington, to learn my way
around and fit myself into a new job all on my own. And for a
girl who came from a small-town relatively innocent
atmosphere, to find that there were 45,000 American soldiers

Wellington women socialising with American marines, Majestic Cabaret, Willis Street, Wellington, c.1942. E. M. Allerdice Collection, Alexander Turnbull Library

roaming the streets of Wellington! It's quite an experience coming from a small place where there were not many men; they're either too young or too old, and here they were *thousands* of them. Americans, Americans!

You could take your pick because they'd come up and they'd say, 'Hiya babe, hiya honey, going my way?' And when you politely said, 'No,' they didn't take any notice. They would take your arm and drag you away and I became very adept at kicking them in the shins. And then I'd wait hopefully for a tramcar to come along to escape.

Inside the shops they used to have the numbers for the military police. If the boys played up you rang the military police and they'd come along and take them away. The military police were not gentle either.

Going to work in the mornings you'd see the filthy conditions of the Wellington streets and footpaths. You came out after the pictures and you'd see the soldiers, sailors, fornicating in the doorways and the next morning there'd be streams of urine and worse—shall I say it? French letters on the footpaths, in the gutters and other unmentionable things, and the city council had not made *one* preparation for the invasion of all these thousands of men. They were expected to use the hotel toilets presumably and they were crowded out. So it was very much going along with your eyes closed.

The Americans were very fond of ice-cream so we developed milkbars that sold milkshakes and ice-cream, the way the Americans liked them. There were three in Cuba

Shake, soda and sundae time for the American marines at the American Red Cross Milkbar, Hotel Cecil, Wellington, c.1943. Gordon Burt Collection, Alexander Turnbull Library

Street, one in Willis Street and there were two on the Quay. And this was sort of a hang-out for the young ones, looking for dates with the Americans and the Americans were looking for dates with girls, and they would ogle one another. 'Halloa babe!' But I wasn't into that.

You were saying that the Americans had tablets . . .

Oh yes, I was talking with some girls at the firm, I worked in the shop, and they were showing me the pills that the Americans had given them to take so that they wouldn't become pregnant. I said to them, 'What is the name of the pills?' and they said sulphanilamide, which had just come on for the treatment of infectious disease, and really didn't prevent pregnancy at all, they were just keeping the girls clean from communicable disease. I told the girls, but they didn't want to believe me—they sincerely thought they were being protected—
they thought I was just being sour.
　The birth-rate soared in New Zealand during the latter part of the war years.
Well, the feller's going overseas isn't he? He's young and he's full of life and he doesn't know what's around the next corner so he's taking his pleasure where he can find it, never mind about the girl, he's going over to Bataan or wherever, being shot at, taken prisoner by the Japs, his life is very short.
You felt very sorry for them. The boys seemed to be so young

'R & R'—a sailor and a soldier stroll on the beach at Oriental Bay with their girlfriends.
Alexander Turnbull Library and Internal Affairs

and so thin and their officers seemed to be middle-aged and fat. I saw it from the view of a nurse and I felt sorry for them yet one has to look after one's self. It's just a town in wartime.

It was very, very difficult in the war years to find accommodation. For the first few months I had a bedsit; actually it was a single room and the walls were very thin between my room and the bedsit next door. They were a strange couple, presumably husband and wife, but certainly partners. He didn't seem to work at all, I don't know how he managed to loaf around the way he did, and she used to go out to work about 10 o'clock at night and come home in the early hours of the morning.
And he would say to her, 'How much did you make tonight?' And she'd pretend she didn't earn very much. 'Come on,' he'd say, 'you've got more than that tucked away, how much have you got?', and then she'd squeal and he'd say, 'Come on, I want it all.'
'You're not going to get it all,' she'd say. And then there'd be another squeal and this was the way it would go on until she'd parted over with all the money that she had on her person. Where she earned it I had no idea—your guess is as good as mine. And do you know what he was doing to her? I found out later by speaking to her. He used to sadistically pinch her, and when she refused to give him money he'd pinch her and pinch her until she couldn't stand any more pinching and she'd part over with the money.

I wouldn't be so rude as to ask her what she was doing and she didn't volunteer the information.

One's eyes are opened, as you're working away you hear the girls talking and lose innocence very rapidly. I was at one stage waitressing and there were some girls there who had 'arrangements' with fellows, every now and again they would say, 'So and so's around,' and they'd be taken out.
There was one girl who was manpowered to a waitressing job and she was very annoyed because she earned more money in her bedsit than she did waitressing. But anyway I didn't worry about those things. What is, is, and that's the way it is and those girls save us a lot of problems.

I found the best way to learn Wellington was to get on a tram and go to various termini, and my favourite one settled to be taking a book and some sandwiches to the Te Aro saltwater baths which were then situated in Oriental Bay round about where Freyberg Pool is now. One for males and one for females. I didn't care for swimming very much so I used to just sunbathe. It was a beautiful place made of timber. The floor was slats so you could see the tide in the water underneath and you'd hear the slap slap slap of the water against the piles and you'd sit there and the sun would shine, read away, get a lovely tan and go back home again to what would be a lonely bedsit.
My husband was away at sea, and I didn't know a soul in Wellington, so I decided to get a job with decent pay and I landed quite a nice job in a munitions factory called Precision

Engineering which was then in Kent Terrace. It was word of mouth that there was a job going so I applied for it and got it. If you managed to get a job that was a reserved occupation the manpower didn't interfere. But you just couldn't take *any* job, it had to be working for the war effort, so anyway I had no problem getting this job with the munitions department. It was a nice job.

The engineering factory was quite different from anything I had ever worked at before. There were six women and a whole factory full of men. The factory itself was sort of dark and cold and dim, full of weird machinery. They have all these lathes moving, and presses coming down bang. There are places that are quite dangerous like the guillotine room where they are cutting up huge sheets of metal. And they've got all these electrical welders going bang, bang, and sparks flying everywhere.

It's quite a challenge and something new. I really enjoyed my time on munitions. The wages were good too.

    The girls were busy sorting and sifting the pins for hand grenades and doing a little bit of welding. And there came a time when the men were asked to produce more trench mortar bomb tails—production was going backwards—I think the total for the day was about 800. The men were laying back a little bit on it so the job was given to the girls who in due course proceeded to put up a good front.

We would take it in turn to work this tremendous machine. It was about a 70-ton press, it breathed fire and dust and heat. It was designed to put vanes on the tail of the bombs. They said it was the largest welder in the Southern Hemisphere. It was divided into two parts—one half, about the size of a very large table, was bedded on the floor very firmly, and the other was above it and there were three wedges which joined when you pulled a lever. In the middle it held an eight-inch bomb tail tube and round that you fed three mortar vanes. Then you pressed the lever and gave it power and it welded 24 nipples instantaneously. It was an *enormous* thing, almost frightening, but we girls learnt and we managed. The assistant handled the red-hot bomb tails as they came out of the welder—we had a long pair of forceps like hospital theatre forceps—you'd lift up these red-hot mortar bomb tails, dip them in an oil and then stack them on pegs on trays. We worked two-hour shifts either side, taking it in turns.

Anyway this particular day Frances said to me, 'Ali would you like to put in a real day's work? The men are being sarcastic about the output of the bomb tails. Would you like to show them once and for all what girls could do?'
'Certainly, I'm on.'
So we started right on the dot of 8 o'clock, spelled each other every second hour and by midday the numbers were getting towards the thousand mark. So after lunch the men started wandering around the factory—the girls were up to something? They were looking at the pile of bomb tails growing higher and higher and not one said a word. They'd all just stare, go away, and another one would come, stare and go

away and by 4 o'clock they were all aware that the girls had well and truly broken the record. We finished at 4.15 with 1200 finished completed bomb tails.
Of course we didn't keep up that every day, but that was the record set for the duration of the war. And as the men came through, not one said 'Well done'—it was just their male ego, they didn't want to be outclassed by a female.
We were tired, dusty, exhausted and hot but we were *triumphant*!

Eventually the boys came home from overseas, and the girls went to their husbands, or found partners and went away to be married, but I was still at the munitions, and then they decided to go on to peace-time production, so in due course there was only two ladies left and we were told we would be finished up.
You do feel a little bit moved over; you worked hard and done a good job . . . oh, well, we knew the war was over and we all had other plans to do.

The end of the war . . .

Well, we had VE Day first and that was quiet for me because I was at the factory then and they didn't give us any time off, it was just another day. So we made up our minds, my husband said, 'If I happen to be ashore at the time,' (strangely enough he was) 'we are going to really celebrate VJ Day when it arrives.'

So we did. We were helping to run a dance in Cambridge Terrace in the United Friendly Society's building, it was called Palm Grove, and my husband was the MC and I helped the pianist and his wife to do the suppers, and we had a thousand people celebrated VJ Day at Palm Grove. Five hundred couples danced away the night and there wasn't one fight or one argument and we had three sittings of supper. There was so little room that they had to take it in turns to dance on the floor and there was rings of people around waiting to take their turn. Absolutely marvellous atmosphere. Everyone laughing and happy, saying what they were going to do as soon as the peace was fixed. I remember dancing with a policeman and he said, 'I can't wait to get out of a uniform.' We all had plans, other plans; mostly for we married ones, it was to find a home.

Yes, we knew about the bombs dropped on Nagasaki and Hiroshima, but when you're celebrating you're just celebrating for yourself, it's all over, we're free, we're free! Six years' effort, it's finished and done with. A wonderful feeling but at the same time there was this atom bomb thing. We all knew that the world had changed somehow and it wasn't for the best.

Peacetime meant the need for bombs came to an end—presses were converted to producing brass and nickel milk tokens for the City Council. Eventually the metals were replaced by plastic and another era arrived. Likewise for Ali. At the end of the war she went back to waitressing, before spending a few months in a factory making radios. Her particular job then was filling cans with hot pitch. She was pregnant at the time and at the end of her fifth month she decided to give up work. There was no one to take her place, she recalls, and this caused a hold-up in the production line. The job was no longer considered fit for a woman, but the male apprentices would have nothing to do with it. It was dirty hot work. The managing director, unable to wait any longer, decided to fill the cans himself. Five minutes after he had started, he poured hot pitch over his hands and burnt himself badly.

'Well that fixed it, it was definitely not a job for a woman. They advertised for a man particularly, and paid him nine pounds per week. I was very annoyed when I heard about it. I had been doing it for four years, getting three pounds per week and suddenly it's not a woman's job it's a man's job and they pay him three times as much. I got my first feminine click, one might say. I was beginning to learn.'

Tepara Mabel Waititi
(née Henare)

*O*f Motatau, Hapu Ngati Te Tarawa, Te Orewai, Ngatihine, Nga Puhi Te Iwi, Mabel and her late husband, the master carver Hori (George) Waititi lived in Motatau, which has always had a predominately Maori population. Their main source of income was a school bus run and a passenger/goods service. They owned a truck and a bus and covered many miles making rural deliveries and transporting school children and others. Until the war George Waititi and his brother-in-law (Mabel's older brother) ran the Henare family delivery business together. During the war Mabel carried it on with the help of a younger brother.

Mabel's was an arranged marriage to George, in August 1939. At the time he was carving the timber for the Waitangi whare runanga. She recalls a relative's comment at the wedding which in hindsight she realises was made to make her aware of what could happen to her . . .

When we got married an uncle of mine said, 'The husband will only have to look at her and she's pregnant. Ngati Porou you know. She comes from big families.'
One auntie had 21, mother comes from a family of 19 and the sisters have 19 each . . . perhaps I'll have big families like them.
And I thought to myself, now, if I have 19 or 21 children how am I going to look after them? I used to cry. I can't look after that many children. Anyhow it happened that I had only four. But somehow I brought up quite a few beside my own.
And that made up for the 19 or 21 children.

It was two years before her first child was born. Tukaki was eight months old and she was 25 when it was inevitable that her husband and her brother Kahukiwi Henare were going to go overseas together with the Maori Battalion.

Unlike many couples in similar circumstances, the Waititis were able to talk about what might happen because of George going to war. Mabel was frank about her fear of him being killed. Likewise he was candid about what he expected if 'the worst' did happen. Amongst other things, it was arranged that Mabel would take over the business while he and Kahu Henare were away.

I didn't like the idea but he was determined he was going to go. I had my fears they might get bombed from the air or torpedoed in the sea and they may not reach their destination. And the other fears I had—he might come back minus one

Mr Cossey, Bob Peeri and Kahukiwi in front of the school bus, 1938

arm, one eye or leg or even both. And then there'd be a lifetime looking after him.

Of course that's why I supposed I married him, 'till death us do part'. I said to him, 'If you do go it looks as if I've got to rear that boy on my own.' Well, he did say that if he does not return then he wants his son to take up carving just like himself and I was to send him to the carving school in Rotorua when he becomes of age.

He regretted that all he had to leave me was our son and his carving tools.

The other thing he said was, 'I know about the First World War' . . . a lot of his relations came back and the wives were already living with others . . .

'If that does happen, I will not have any grudge against you because I left you in the first place, but if I do return I want my son back.'

He was only eight months old when he left and when he came back our son was five years and three weeks. He was already ready for school.

Anyhow, George, he wanted to go. All his friends and cousins were. He thought it was his duty.

So he did go over.

When my mother and I went to see my brother and my husband off at Palmerston she was saying, 'There are some there with really sad faces and I don't think those will come back. But with these two, well, they look really pepped up,' and she said, 'I think they're going to come back.'

Mabel (centre) in the prize-winning Motatau Cultural Group, 1935

The wedding of Mabel Henare and Hori (George) Waititi, August 1939

Now and again I feel sorry for my mother. Sometimes she doesn't come out of her room so I'd go over and find her crying with a prayer book beside her.
And I said to her, 'Oh well, we'll keep working. That'll be the best thing we can do.'
And it was really heartbreaking to see our son because he fretted for weeks and weeks when my husband left. He wouldn't eat.
So that put the worry on me. He really worried me. I had to take him to the doctor about twice a week because of his not eating.

George (far left) and fellow carvers at Tukaki meeting house, 1940

But my husband is away so young brother and I had to run our business which was a school bus run—passenger and general goods. So I turned round to driving our truck or the bus, and that helped by working. I think it took a lot off my mind by working.
But wherever I went, my son will not stay home. He refused to stay back. So he goes with me whatever I'm on, bus or truck. Several times he fell asleep, and then the next thing I found he was getting down on the floor of the cab to sleep and I thought, 'Oh well if he's more comfortable down there, let it be.' But coming in and out of the truck, it's dirty, you know? Farmers' gates and what-not, it's not clean. But still he puts his blanket down. Mum had to wash it after a day's trip.
Before we leave in the morning I get a blanket and a pillow for him when he wants a sleep and some food so he can munch

Mabel with her son Tukaki, 1943

away every time he feels hungry.
And I think that helped him, he started to forget about fretting. Anyhow he grew up either on the truck or the bus and he seemed to have known everybody around.
And of course there was only one language he spoke and it was Maori. If anybody spoke to him in English he wouldn't know what they're talking about.

I first got my licence in 1937.
I was fortunate that I was the first Ngatihine woman to get a car licence, a heavy traffic and a motor omnibus licence, so I did enlist in the Red Cross as a Red Cross driver, but my mother refused to look after my son.
She said, 'You were left to look after that son, I will not look after him for you.'
So I had to carry on with our business which was a very heavy task—leaving home six o'clock in the morning. Go and pick up all the cream cans—so many byroads to Hikurangi—and drive the cream lorry with all the cans, we had 42 suppliers. You got to know all the numbers from each stand, or else if you put a wrong one down you find a furious farmer the next round.
And as well as unloading the cream, because the dairy factory had their own shop, they used to order the flour by the 100 pound bags and the sugar in 70 pound bags and the butter in 20 pound boxes. So if ten farmers ordered the same thing you've got a *big* load to take back.
The people at the shops were very helpful. I had a fifteen-year-

Riuroa Henare, Mabel's mother, 1964

old boy with me who did a lot of the heavy lifting but sometimes I get wild that I, a woman, am doing a man's job.

One day I came back from Hikurangi, arrived back about half past two or three, and was told I had to go and pick up a load of ten big sacks of chaff and bran from the railway station and drive way to the back of this farm and unload them.
And when I get over there, there's a message for me to bring a hay sweep for a farmer. So had to load that, bring it back to the farmer and there's a message to hop on the bus to pick up the passengers down at the railway station!
It's about half past eight before I finished and I was really dog tired. And then six o'clock the next morning, I'm on the depot again.

I was unloading a 44 gallon petrol drum one day — the thing is there standing level with the floor of back of the truck in the tray, so I wheeled it around and then I felt a crack in my chest.
Oooh, it was painful! So I went home and rushed up to the hospital. I told them, 'I've got to be back on that truck again in the morning,' so they put a very wide sticking plaster on. It was good, but as I was coming down the steps I realised my son, who was two and a half years old, was still on the breast. So I went back. 'Aw . . . there's something wrong.' 'What?' And I said, 'My son is still on the breast!'
What we did . . . cut some holes for the nipples, through the

Mabel, the truck driver on the dairy factory run

plaster. Of course he was quite happy with that!
And the next day I was on the cream run again and it's a long way, probably with all the runs through the byroads and that, about I suppose it'd be about 72 miles one way.

The bridges were one-way bridges of course so I could see this chap coming on the little truck and I could see he had no brakes, I could see him straining, so I stopped and we *just* missed by about a couple of inches and he hopped out of his truck, he was a Pakeha chap, and he abused me and swore, so I took my hat off and my hair fell down and he said, 'I'm sorry, I'm sorry I thought you were a man.'
Because I had a combination overall and I had my brother's hat on.

So were people looking down their noses at you because you were a woman driving a truck?

No. As a matter of fact they were really appreciative because they knew that a lot of the ones that stayed back, they had no licence, so you can't just pick on them to drive.
One day on my way to Hikurangi, one of the army, don-Rs they called them then, [dispatch riders] on the motorbike, comes and stops, and this chap tells me there's 500 vehicles on the way. There's been a Japanese scare from Opua up to Matauri Bay.
So next thing we met these vehicles coming one after another with the army trucks, bren carriers and troop carriers and all

sorts . . . they were passing that fast I started to vomit, like
seasick. So I drove my truck on the side of the road and I
asked the chap that was with me, 'How many have gone past?'
He said only 90, *there's still 410 to come*!
So we were late that day for about an hour and a half.
I couldn't even drive for a while.

How did people feel about the Japanese?

Well, they were all scared about it.
At one time there was a Japanese called Jack Sato, he came
around and pretended that he was a wool broker. Then one
day my mother said I'd better take a photo and he ran away.
He said, 'No no no no photo!'
He must have been a spy after all . . .
There was a young Japanese student that came out touring
about three or four years ago and my son-in-law picked him
up and he stayed for nine months with them. It was raining
and he picked him up at Kerikeri . . . he was a very nice
young man,
but there was no love between them during the war, not up
our way anyway, not with Japanese then. We thought if the
Japanese came . . . well, everybody had gone to the war and
left the place empty eh?

Did you hear from your husband?

Yes. The correspondence was pretty good. My husband and my brother used to write quite often but sometimes the letters had parts blackened out. Things I suppose they're not supposed to say.

But the other thing we did was sending parcels—we sent individual parcels wrapped in paper and we got back, the word back from Egypt, 'Please wrap the parcels up in linen and sew them up.'

They said a lot of the things went astray, the soldiers did not get them.

So myself and a cousin of mine Ada Walker, we looked after the money for the Maori Patriotic Committee in our area, and were responsible for sending the parcels over for the soldiers. This chap, Mr Tudhope gave us a corner in the Bargain Stores in Whangarei so we sat there and parcelled for our soldiers. We had to put everything inside and then sew unbleached linen, wrapped around the tins.

We had 24 in the first lot but as time went on—I remember the last lot we sent there were only nine. A lot of them had been killed. Some of the husbands died and the Ngatihine tribe lost quite a lot of young men.

When the word is received that a soldier had died, we all go to that particular marae, if they got a marae, or to their home, and help the ones that lost a soldier.

But the thing is . . . they're crying over just the photo, and they know the body will never be returned. Aue, that really

George, Narrow Neck Camp, Auckland, 1943

saddened us. That saddened me most—see them crying just
over a photo.
At the marae, at the homes, not long after they put memorial
stones up with the names of the soldiers that were killed.
Children. Parents. Father. Died over there.
I was very worried. My husband was wounded twice. I got a
telegram from the Minister, I think Jones was the Minister
then,
saying that he's been wounded but wait for further word.
That was quite good. Then next thing you receives a letter
from him. My husband was saying, when they've gone into an
attack . . . when they come out, the first thing they look for is
their relations.
And of course having my brother and my uncle there and my
cousin Jim Henare and all, you know, worried about each
other when they get back to camp.
Was quite sad in a way. Hmm.

But I had a feeling that my husband would come back because
during his final leave he went back home and his father did
prayers on him, with our son and he said, 'I think you're
going to come back.'
It's the same as Jim Henare.
They had a big gathering and the rituals at Motatau marae
before he left and the elders said to him, 'Leave your marae
walking on your feet and you will return walking on
your feet.'

When war broke out in 1939 Jim's father, Tau Henare, said to Jim, 'Go and enlist. Go to the war,' to pay his debt, because he was one of the many who said 'yes' for the Maoris to go to World War One. 'If you have to pay by your blood, let it be.' So Jim enlisted.

He was telling me when he got wounded the second time—he said, 'Well Father, I think your debt is already paid. Let me go home.'

He was wounded three times, but the thing is, he did come back.

They arrived back January 1946. I had to go down to Cape Runaway because he was told that he's got to see his own first. My mother was happy when she knew they were on their way. She made us laugh. When she heard that the Maori Battalion was going to come back to Kaikohe she went with one of the boys on our truck to Dargaville, got six sacks of toheroas and on the way the inspector stopped her.

'You've got too many toheroas,' he said. 'Oh,' she said, 'I went to get some toheroas for these people that went over to fight for you. They are coming back, they need a feed of toheroas.' So they let her come with the toheroas for the reception at Kaikohe. I thought she was game!

We went from there to Cape Runaway and after that we went from marae to marae down to this side of Opotiki, before we came home. There were tangis at every marae. Oh it was sad—sad for the mothers, and the wives, who had lost their sons over there. At one marae, seven went in the original lot

Mabel's family after a service for local Maori Battalion soldiers on their final leave

and not one came back. There were expressions of sorrow all the time. I think we went on to about six maraes, and spent about a day at each marae up to the last lot and it was sad to see, especially some of the mothers had got old and crying. Seeing the ones that lost their beloved ones but still happy to receive the others.

When the soldiers . . . there were about 30 being welcomed on the marae at Kauae Tangohia (especially down the coast they have seats further down the marae) they come so far, and while they were standing there one of my sisters-in-law said to my son, 'Can you pick your father?'
He said, 'Yes, over there.'
So he walked out, went up, grabbed hold of his leg. And my husband just looked down—oh just another boy grabbing his leg . . . I saw him looking at the people in front of our wharenui, then he saw me and he realised. He said to Colonel Awatere, 'This must be my son.'
We all laughed when we saw him picking him up after about five minutes. He didn't know him, but his son knew by the photographs who he was.

Mabel, how did it go being with your husband and your boy?

Well, when we went up north George was alright for the first couple of months. But after a while I could see that he couldn't stand him and I think it's just because he didn't bring him up

anyhow when we got our second son, it really showed up then. He had more time for Kahu, our second son,
and it went on and on and on and I thought to myself I'd better have a talk with him.
He said he did not realise that it was happening.
The other thing was my mother really loved the first one and one day I heard her say, 'You're just a troublemaker' to the second one.
She could see what was happening. Anyhow when we had a good talk about it everything was ironed out.
But I was pleased he came back with my brother because they did all the driving so I didn't have to go driving. I was quite happy but soon after that I was nominated for our post office so that's where I worked for 31½ years. So from one job to another.

Those war years, I don't think they really were the best of my life because I had to do a lot of a man's work that's what made me feel sad about them taking all the men away and leaving us women to do a lot of work. It made me aware what other people are doing too. Because they were suffering the same. I didn't think it affected me—only the absence of my husband.
As a matter of fact it did make me appreciate that I did like working for my community. My parents were brought up working for the community—and my grandmother—they all worked for the community, so it made me aware it's my turn to do the same.

Mabel, on retirement from Motatau Post Office, 1981, after 31½ years. *Northern News*, Kaikohe

While her husband was overseas she managed to get them a house of their own. 'There were some cheap homes going so I got this house for us, because we were living with my mother before he left. Of course it didn't last that long, being a cheap house, so we had to build another one.'

She thinks of those post-war years as a struggle and wonders whether the Maori Battalion servicemen should have got more assistance in re-settling and more direct help for the education of their children, which she considered so essential.

But Mabel remembers mostly how strong the bonds were, post-war, between the men, especially her husband and her brother. They often talked about their comrades. It always surprised her, considering the contribution the Battalion made to the war effort, that there was only ever one Maori VC. 'I thought with all the praise and whatnot about the Maori Battalion, what they did, and only got one VC and that was to a dead comrade.'

Rita Graham
(née Watts)

Rita and Alan, an accountant, married in January 1939 after a two-and-a-half-year engagement. They were able to do this when Alan suddenly got a rise in salary at his job at the Auckland Savings Bank. As was the custom at the time, Rita gave up her department store position to become a full-time wife and home-maker.

Although there had been rumours of an impending war for some months, it seemed remote to Rita . . . something that was happening on the other side of the world, not in her small contented corner of it. Rita wasn't particularly interested in war, however Alan's feelings about it were uncompromising.

Before they had even become engaged, Alan had made it very clear to her that in the event of a war he would be a conscientious objector. War and killing were against his religious beliefs. They never discussed the subject of pacifism beyond that until war was finally and officially declared in September.

Alan said to me, 'You do realise that if war were to come about, I would not go?'

And I just said, 'That's alright.'

I wasn't really interested in the fact that he wasn't going to go to war. I don't think I took too much notice of it. I'm pretty sure I didn't. My life was taken up with being married and thinking it was wonderful living on Cheltenham Beach swimming all day. As long as I got home and cooked the dinner at night I had fulfilled my obligations. And I thought that was just great. I was aware of the rumours of war but it was in the future and I wasn't going to worry about that too much.

We had our first son in 1941, and in 1942 in July our daughter was born.

And while I was in that nursing home, Alan received a paper asking him to present himself for a medical, prior to doing military service. Alan felt no reason for him not to attend his medical although he was opposing war. He thought it was important that he not be let off in any way because of any disability, or reason, that he couldn't serve his military service. He felt it was important that he be classed A-1, and then make his protest.

Women didn't challenge their husbands in those days. I'm talking about 56 years ago. I'm pretty sure I didn't.

But I thought a lot about what he was doing. I hadn't any desire to become a pacifist then. I really don't know when I became one. But then, I really think I was wrapped up in my

Rita and Alan on their wedding day, 20 January 1939

family—I had a loving, wonderful husband. A man who was very highly principled. Everything he did was with the highest motives.

What concerned me, more than anything, was the way people would look at me—how neighbours would look at me if Alan didn't go to war. I was a little bit ashamed.

I didn't know how I was going to cope with this as it got nearer, and nearer. It was alright while I could block it out, but somewhere along the line it had to be faced.

And I was in that nursing home when he got a call-up to present himself for military service and he refused to go and he went before a small tribunal, said his wife was in the nursing home with a young baby, and was granted a one-month extension. In those days it was customary to stay in the nursing home for two weeks. You stayed in bed for ten days and you got up for the last four and it was a lovely holiday. But I went home so weak, almost unable to stand, and tried to cope with this young baby and a little boy of 18 months.

Yes, life wasn't particularly easy at the time.

So at the end of that one-month extension when my little baby would then be six weeks old, Alan was required to go to the police station.

I have the feeling it was early evening round about four or five o'clock and I remember Alan taking *the* most enormous suitcase, the biggest we had, I couldn't lift it off the ground and I don't think he could either.

'What have you got in it?' I said.

Rita and Alan (on the right) on their honeymoon, Tauranga, February 1939

'I'm going for a long time, I'm taking books.'
He had one change of clothes and his books.
    So I left Alan at the police station.
They had taken his tie, taken his shoe laces . . . Alan had been
a professional businessman—the manager of a small branch—
always with the collar and tie at the bank.
And so I saw Alan with an open-neck shirt, and they took his
wedding ring,
and I felt pretty sad
but I was with another girl who was seeing her husband also
being left behind and the two of us walked from Princes Street
police station to Balmoral Road and Dominion Road because
we'd both been crying so much we didn't feel we could get on
a tram and go home.
And I remember getting home and not having any milk to
feed the baby and being in a pretty desperate situation.
Obviously we found some Karilac or something for the baby.
    The next day I remember taking every stitch of clothing
that Alan had ever had on and boiling up the copper and
having a really good wash-up—the lines full of clothes—
knowing that physical work was going to get some of this out
of my system.
None of us knew how long it was going to be. All the people
whose husbands went to the war had no idea.
I think that's probably one of the hardest things to come to
terms with—
the indefiniteness of it all.

This was a difficult time for his mother and for my mother. His mother was a widow and people in the street remarked, 'What's your son doing?' 'He's in the Pacific,' was a satisfactory answer for her. She could not bring herself to say he was a defaulter. She couldn't bring herself to say he's a conscientious objector.
She had three sons. One was a naval officer and one was in the air force, but she could not face up to really what I know to be her most loved son, the one that had such high principles, and he could not fight for his country. She was so embarrassed and my mother also.

It took time for me to absorb the fact that I had to be loyal for Alan too.
I know it took a long time.
When people said, 'Where's your husband?' I would dodge the issue, skirted around it. I'm quite sure that I was running with the hares and hunting with the hounds.
I don't think that anyone had any idea of the pressures that were put on people to be behind the war effort.
And I need to say this because I think it's important—what happened at the bank was very interesting. All the big firms in the city were writing big advertisements, 'We are 100% behind the war effort.'
The Auckland Savings Bank was not in a position to do that because Alan had refused to go to the war and was still working there. And I'm quite sure that was a stumbling block

because the bank manager was a prominent Methodist . . . the manager gave him the opportunity to resign but Alan said, 'I feel I have done my best and I will not resign.'
Then when Alan finally got a conviction the manager said, 'I have no alternative but to sack you,' and from that moment on the bank was one hundred percent behind the war effort.
I remember that.

There was one man at that time working at the bank who had a very bad hearing problem and was not able to work on the counter. I'm very happy to give his name, it was Campbell Paterson, he died a week ago.
He went to the manager and said, 'It has been our custom when a boy has gone overseas from the bank to give him a gold watch and we'd like to do that for Alan.'
The manager was furious—an insult to the boys who had gone overseas—dreadful to even suggest it.
So Campbell went back and amongst the group he talked to was a man who'd come back from the war having lost his eye. And that man went up and spoke to the bank manager and said, 'I support Campbell—let's give him a gold watch.' And he still would not have it. So Campbell then went amongst the staff and discussed with them what they could do and I know the largest amount given by any one person was a shilling. There was threepences and sixpences, they took up a collection and all the years that Alan was in detention, those three years, they paid me ten shillings a week into my bank account.

Far more than any gold watch and of so much greater value for me.

    I'm sure that that tremendous support gave me the ability to cope with what I should have coped with years before.
I don't think you can even pass this on to anyone who hasn't experienced the pressures to support the war effort. In some ways I could liken it to raising funds for the America's Cup. Every paper and every magazine you pick up . . . 'Support the Americas Cup.' Well this is how it was during that war. 'We are behind the war effort.' 'You must do your bit!' 'We may not be here and live the lives we have if we don't support the war effort.' That pressure that was put on the community, was put on the churches too, and therefore we did not get support from the church.
There was antagonism. But, there again, I suppose the church could not be one hundred percent for the war effort. They had a group of rebels who were saying they wouldn't go.
I have a long association with the Methodist Church from way back in my father's time. The church was the whole of our lives. Morning, noon and night and every day of the week. I'm grateful for that. Very grateful for the background that I'd had. But the church didn't grow with the times. I can remember one man, and one man only, coming to me from the Dominion Road church saying . . . he called me as I was going home from church one day, 'Rita, while I hate pacifism I have no reason to hate the pacifists.'
That stayed with me and I will never forget it. It was one of

the most generous things he could have done. He stood alone to come and say that to me.
Having said that I must go on to another episode in my life. When my little girl, Heather, was a week off being 12 months old, I was making arrangements to go and see Alan. I could only go and visit when I could get a ride and there was an opportunity coming up that meant I could take Heather down to see him. I'm going out, making these arrangements and mother said, 'Look, it's a nasty day, why don't you take Stuart and go to your friend's for lunch and I'll mind Heather at home?'
Well that made sense, so I did.
And I remember coming home in the tram from Orakei and I found a commotion at home. Heather had died in the pram. She'd been asphyxiated by a little strap that was in the big old-fashioned pram and mother hadn't seen her. She thought she was alright until she saw some bubbles. And Heather had died. Mother had a heart attack there straight away. A terrible situation.

    I rang my friend Campbell Paterson at the bank, told him what had happened.
He came out to me and the memory I have is clear today, silly little trivial things that you keep in your mind. A shoebox filled with three bunches of primroses and three bunches of violets. 'The typists sent these to you.'
And he said he'd some money he'd gathered up. What could he do—what could he do to help me?

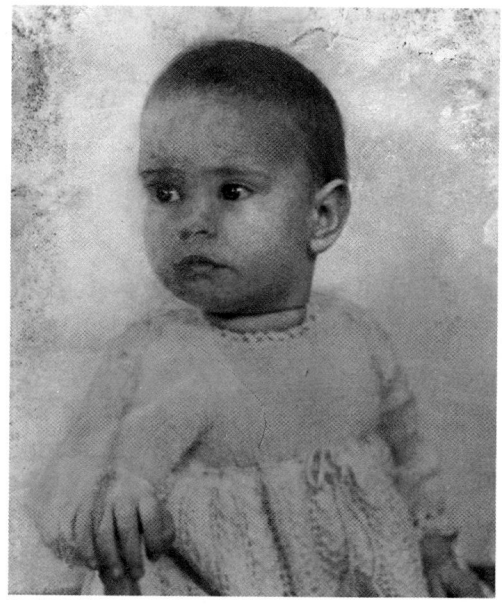

Photograph of Heather Mary Graham, taken the day before she died, 28 July 1943

Well somebody got in touch with the chaplain of the church and I have to say I'm very grateful to him. He got Alan home for three days. That was compassionate leave.
We had Heather at home, so that he could see her, because he hadn't seen her since she was a month old.

Alan came home for three days and what mixed feelings I had. I remember feeling overjoyed that he was home . . . so happy . . . and yet so miserable because it was to see the funeral of his daughter. The funeral had to be held at home. He was not allowed to mix with any crowd and he had to report to the police station every day and it was very brief.

It was expressed to me, I'm certain it never came from the person who said it, but it was expressed to me that perhaps Heather's death was a punishment.

You, you've got to understand there were people in the community here whose sons had been killed. Sons who'd been maimed and perhaps not killed.
I have to look at it that way now.
They, the community, was suffering, terrible pain, terrible pain. Mine was a different pain, mine was a different suffering, that was all.

I didn't see it, but I'm sure Alan cried inside. Bitterly disappointed that this little girl that he was so thrilled to have was not there any more. Bitterly disappointed.
But he didn't show it to me.
Perhaps we, who can cry more easily, did not feel it as deeply?
Even though I was the mother, I wonder whether I felt it as

Heather's grave, Waikaraka Cemetery

deeply as he did. He just doesn't have the ability to express it. Well, at the end of three days Alan went back to prison, and I suppose this is one of the most difficult times in my life. I was very distressed. Very distressed.

All the detainees were permitted to write one sheet of paper as a letter. They could write both sides. And I think there were some there that could probably win a prize for the smallest writing that you could ever get because it was censored and they'd write as much as they could on a page. And I looked forward to those letters—they came once a week. As soon as Alan got back, I'm waiting for his letter and the mail comes and I open the letter because I needed then some support. There's a little bit of scrappy paper torn out of a book. 'Sorry I've lost my privileges. Can't write for a month. Love Alan.' He'd lost his privileges.

And I think I have to say this because it is important. I hated him. I really did. How could he do that to me? The *one* thing I wanted was a letter and he'd lost his privileges.

Blow his privileges and his feelings!

When I look back . . . oh I needed that support then, I really did and I didn't have it. I didn't admit to the anger till many many years later. But I know it was there now, having talked it out—I know I was angry because I felt that he'd not considered me at all.

I probably was egged on a little by my mother who'd have said, 'Where was your husband?' She'd wonder why he'd gone

Hautu Detention Camp—photographs taken against camp rules

on a hunger strike. She'd think he'd already made a protest by going into detention anyway.

I probably avoided writing rather than say something bad that might have upset him, because he was in a difficult situation too. I mean, he'd been sent to the 'bad boys' camp'. Hautu was the place where you were sent. So I wouldn't want to make things any worse for him

I think I want to tell you this too . . . and I hope this will not upset Alan—when I've mentioned it before he feels I don't put the right emphasis in the right place so let's hope I can do it this time . . .

Alan is a very methodical person. Detention provided for him ideal circumstances. He woke at six, the ablutions were held and seven o'clock it was breakfast. Eight o'clock you went to work, lunch was at 12 and you went through till your dinner at night and then there was time before you were put in your hut and the doors were closed and lights out at nine o'clock, or something like that. Now those conditions were ideal for Alan.

He missed the family *terribly* but he did use that time very well. There were university lecturers, the top thinking teachers were all in Hautu and Alan made use of everything that was available to him. He studied Spanish, cost accounting. Alan was not happy there, he did not like it but I know that it suited that type of nature that he had . . . so that that period was not entirely wasted.

And I have to say here, that the whole of that experience of

Alan Graham (left) with three fellow detainees, Hautu Detention Camp

Alan being in detention became a very positive one for me.
I remember on one occasion being in the city and waiting to catch a tram home and a woman said something to me about the war, don't recall what she said but I remember coming out and saying, 'My husband's a conscientious objector and he's in detention,' very positively.
I believe the whole change in my life took place once I came out and made that statement. Because it was a positive statement. I wasn't having to hide it. I wasn't on the back foot. I was on the front foot and I think I probably felt very much better and I felt loyal to Alan. And I think it enabled me to change the whole of my life.

I had abuse after I made that statement. Not on that occasion but sometimes I got abused. People were very rude, they would talk about 'conchies'. We had a white feather, on more than one occasion, posted in an envelope. I took a while to cope with that. Funny, just a silly little white feather in an envelope is nothing. But what it signified, being a coward, was difficult sometimes to accept.

I had a very aggressive neighbour who would report me, probably once a month, to the post office and say why wasn't I out working? They'd never asked me to work with two small children—actually she didn't have anyone away at the war at all—but she would go out there and throw an empty milk bottle through my mother's sunporch window. Very distressing for my mother who just wished to get along nicely with all the neighbours. Hard for her to come to terms with that sort of thing.

But that was the pressure going on during those war years.

It was a struggle, but I was paid by the government while he was in prison. I had a pound a week for myself and ten shillings for each child. Now Heather died on a Wednesday and they stopped me that half a week so I only got five shillings. I mean, it was a pittance. Alan got what he paid into the bank when he was sacked, nothing more. But he had that money behind him so he said while we're there, best pay the rent because my mother needed that. She needed that.

I grew vegetables, I also grew cyclamen, I grew some gladioli and sold the flowers.

And here again we go back to the bank.

Campbell came to me and said, 'At night time when your children are in bed and asleep could you fill some stamp packets for me?'

Yes I could. I remember I took stamps out of envelopes. I had these laid out all over the table, and put them up into packets. I may have been paid a penny ha'penny a packet. I'm really a bit vague about that.

I don't recall having a lot of close friends with people my own age during the war.

There were occasions when I went to the Quaker meeting house in Mt Eden Road where some of us with small children got together. None of us had transport, none of us had money to go far although it wasn't expensive in the tram.

I think we probably found we were happy to lead just our little quiet lives. As far as I was concerned there was no social life. I was not acceptable really out in that world. I had nothing in common with the people out there. It was alive with sailors. It was alive with people who were supporting the war effort and I really felt very much more comfortable at home. I think I was just a very domesticated person. I did not go out at night. Partly that would be because I was living with my mother and she did have quite strong views at that time that if you had children you were expected to stay home and look after them. This was well before the days when anyone thought of sharing babysitting facilities.

But I had really a very quiet time and that was my choice. Avoiding conflict probably. It may have been magnified in my mind—I thought everybody was against me because of Alan's stand.

I must say it's wonderful today to be able to come out, without any qualms, and talk about it.

    After the death of Heather I went twice to Hautu. Once I was offered a ride. I was very grateful for that ride. I couldn't have gone any other way . . .

There were about six or seven other wives there—and I remember quite a lot of us were in one big open hall and we sneaked off into a corner or a side. And of course we had the children running in and out and I remember very clearly my

little Stuart coming in saying that the supervisor said, 'Go back to your mummy.'
They kept us very much in that environment. We had perhaps two hours and then that would be the end. I was always so pleased . . . I gained tremendous strength from talking to Alan and I knew he did too. The link was very important. Wonderful. You'd gone through a fair amount of trouble to make it there and that was just great. Yes, the trip home was a fairly quiet one.

I had that ability to go back home and recall things and get them firmly implanted in my mind so I could live with that until one knew when the next time was going to be. And in actual fact there wasn't a next time.
What happened was that about a week before VJ Day, these boys were taken from the detention camp into the office and appeared before a little three-man tribunal. And Alan came out classified as a genuine conscientious objector, after three years.
And so the war ended and Alan was home within two or three days. Home very quickly.
That caused a little disturbance and quite a strong ripple amongst the community. How did they let them out so quickly!

I know that I only look at that war situation through a pacifist's eyes, and one doesn't always remember what the people were going through who had people away at the war. They never knew whether, or when, they would come back. I always knew Alan would.

I don't think I ever thought it would be easy, but I knew he was going to come back whole, complete and that we would get together.

    I expected them to keep him for much longer after the war ended than in actual fact happened.

I remember very well how I felt. We had 15 pounds in the bank, that's all we had, and I booked a room at Parakai House in Helensville for Alan and I and Stuart to go up and spend a weekend, I don't think it can have been any more.

And we went up there and I thought, this will be a most wonderful time—we will get to know each other,

but unfortunately it didn't work out quite like that, because on the very first day Alan got talking to a man who showed some interest in what he had done and talked of the possibility of giving him a job. So Alan spent three days walking round Helensville streets with this man trying to prove that he could do the job, to prove that he would be worth employing. And Stuart and Rita came home very disappointed. And the job never did eventuate.

How interesting to look back now and remember that time.

    There were difficulties. There were difficult times.

Stuart would more often than not say, 'I don't want you, I want mummy.' Even at five.

Alan is a quiet, quiet person and he found it very hard to

Rita with her son, Stuart, and her mother, Gertrude Watts, c.1947

come home and not be really accepted. He'd been away for three years, Stuart really didn't remember him. He'd seen him three times in that time and I think partly due to the loss of our baby, Stuart had had all the attention he could ever have from my mother and myself and suddenly there was an intrusion.

I can remember disappointment on Alan's part. Looking forward so much to coming home. It wasn't easy.

We tried to have another child and it took me a long time before I could conceive again. The thyroid had become overactive after Heather's death and there were lots of problems there. Eventually I had a second son. There's seven years between Stuart and Ian.

For me looking back, at this distance . . . what am I talking about . . . over 50 years, I can only feel the positive results. The strength I gained by the stand I had to make to be positive about pacifism—that gave me the strength to cope with a severe hearing impairment.

I look back now and think the Rita that was before would not have coped as well. The disability would have been a disaster to me. But somewhere I gained great strength and I have to pay great tribute to a very loving husband. A man of whom I'm extremely proud.

    I did my talking well after the war—well after the war.

    I doubt I even told Alan my feelings until years later. I remember him saying to me, 'I was shocked when I heard you

telling somebody how you felt about me not writing to you
when Heather died.' He said, 'I never realised that.' He
never realised. See, he is a quiet man and doesn't express
his feelings.

We can't have two talkers in the family. When I tell him now
how I felt about those bad years—how I hated him because of
what I was suffering—he can't believe that that was how it
would affect me. He's not as volatile as I am.

But he understands now that I want to discuss it—the
difficulties. He now knows. He would discuss more today with
me than he ever would have in those years when he always
made the decisions.

I had given myself over to him. He was prepared to take over
all the necessities of life, prepare for me, care for me, provide
for me. That was the way we were.

That was the way we were. But there's a closeness now that was
not there before. Yes.

    See, to my generation . . . there were so many things you
couldn't talk about. You had to keep quiet. You couldn't talk
about sex. You couldn't talk about illness . . . my mother would
say 'Cancer' in very hushed tones. Oh, so many things weren't
talked about. Wicked. Wicked.

And of course, once you *can't* talk about something you get
the wrong end of the stick. You imagine it.

Possibly I imagined things were happening when maybe
they weren't.

Wartime, especially, was a period of secrecy. The secret . . . it couldn't be talked about, and that's not me. I had to talk things out. I had to. And since I've been able to do that, nothing will frighten me again in my life.

Immediately after the war Alan was manpowered to work in a butter factory but his intention was to return to accountancy. He applied for many positions, always stating that he was a conscientious objector who had been in detention for his beliefs. His applications were invariably rejected. Finally, he was employed by an accountant who happened to be an admirer of pacifist Ormond Burton. Many of the company's clients were returned servicemen, but this created no problem and Alan stayed with the firm until he got an interesting offer in 1952. The United Nations Relief and Work Agency for Palestine Refugees were looking for an accountant from New Zealand to fill a position in Beirut for six months.

Alan's decision to go overseas left Rita once again on her own with the children, but when his contract was renewed they were reunited in Beirut, where they stayed and worked for 23 years. Ironically Alan found himself in a war zone after all the years of resistance.

With the silences and secrets now in the past, how does Rita regard the war period? 'I say it was the most important time of my life because of what I gained from it. And I am as convinced today as I ever was that war solves no problems, just creates conflict and bitterness. I have yet to be shown a situation where war has solved a problem.'

Neva Clarke McKenna

(née Morrison) MBE

Neva *lives alone out on the picturesque peninsula of Mangonui, surrounded by her many books, her dairies, papers and the research she does for her articles and books on local and regional history.*

She has thought a lot about her wartime experiences, and has talked and written about some of them over the years. The implication is that the peace of mind she might have expected post-war was, initially, elusive. She experienced two difficult and ultimately unsatisfying marriages. But the impression today is of a woman that has taken herself in hand. Despite her warning, 'Don't waste worry . . . there are more important things to do,' you get the feeling that Neva has talked seriously to herself over the past 50 years, and whilst the feelings remain, as red-hot as ever, the pain is comfortably under control. There is a healthiness about the way she finds wartime friends, and memories, are as necessary to her today as they were then.

Neva started work in 1936 as a secretary, having taken the commercial course at Gisborne High School. Post-war, she resumed her secretarial work when she was requested to work in the Prime Minister's Office. When war broke out she was a typist in the Public Service. Eventually she served overseas in the Clerical Division of the New Zealand WAAC (1943–1946). She was in the first group of female office staff sent overseas and had three years in Italy at Administrative HQ. She was promoted and commissioned as 2nd Subaltern and put in charge of secretaries throughout Italy. She was always relatively close to the front—at one stage, just eight miles behind the front line.

Neva at 19, Gisborne, 1939

I was engaged when I was 18, and my fiancé went into the air force—too young—had to get his parents' permission. He went to England, then to North Africa, and he was immediately killed—bombing over Benghazi. That was in 1942.
I was devastated.
I'll never forget the phone ringing, and my mother answered the phone, 'Oh, just a minute,' and she called my father.
I thought, 'Funny, oh, I don't like the sound of that.'
So Dad took the message from Geoff's father to say that Geoff had been killed. And I stood, and I screamed and screamed and screamed and screamed.
Next day I went to work at the Drill Hall helping with the

Neva's fiancé Geoff, aged 20, Napier, 1940. He was killed two years later in an air force bombing exercise over Benghazi

medical boards for men being called up for army service. That was probably good—but I had to cope with it. I mean, you just had to. No alternative.
I live with that, even now . . . I still wear Geoff like a second skin.

    That experience gave me a basis for the rest of my life. It made me able to accept things that would have upset me a lot more had I not been through it. I learned then to tuck the bad things away in a compartment in my mind, and very seldom open the door. I could think about them, but not let them take me over.
I had a friend in the same situation, and she immediately had a nervous breakdown. I decided I wasn't going to be like that—I've a tremendous amount of doggedness in me.

I had come from Gisborne, which was a—what should I say?—a *lively* place. Cut off as you know . . . a great party place. And when I left high school I was just a pain, I was so shy, and I decided at 16 that the only person who could do anything about that shyness was myself, and I joined a ballroom dancing class. Mildred Hamilton's Ballroom Dancing Class. I biked into town on a Tuesday night at half past seven, parked my bike against the kerb and I walked up the stairs—brown linoleum nibbled at the edges as if by rats—and I looked into an enormous room—it had mirrors all around the bottom of the wall so you could see what you were doing wrong with your feet. And I thought—'I've got to run away. I can't bear it.'

Across on the far side of the room there were four or five people who looked as frightened as I was, and I thought, 'If, if I can get across the floor to them, I might be all right.' I managed it, and that night we learned the quarter turn and the natural turn and reverse turn. All of us were scared. And I've never been shy since that day. Never. Never never never.

We began going to all the dances. You know, there'd be eight or ten of us and we would go to the Golf Club ball, and the Hunt Club ball, and I knew a lot of the young farmers and went to the dances in their beautiful woolsheds all done up with fern fronds. Some of them had sprung floors. I danced with the young farmers and with their fathers who whizzed you around in fast waltzes. The mothers made wonderful suppers. I knew all the town boys because I worked with some of them, and I was also involved with the surf club, because I swam, so I knew all the surf club boys. They were a very bright lot.

My older sister and I went to a lot of parties, and we were very, very social, very involved, and we drank a little too much Gold Top beer, perhaps. That was what I came from to go into the army overseas. A lot of the girls had come from very sheltered backgrounds, but Gisborne's isolation made us like a big family making its own fun. And I know that wherever I went, I met Gisborne people. Girls from Christchurch, Auckland, etc. used to say, 'You awful Gisborne people. Wherever you go there's a little mob of you sort of hugging one another.'

And it was true. I remember being on board ship, going to Italy, and I looked from the deck I was on down onto another deck and I saw a fellow called George Selves from Gisborne. I called, 'Hello George!' And *three* Georges from Gisborne waved back to me. It could never have happened with a Christchurch girl or an Auckland girl.

You see, those people could be lost, but nobody from Gisborne could be lost. We all loved each other to pieces. Even if we weren't friends in Gisborne, you know how it is . . . meet a stranger from your hometown in London and they're an immediate friend.

That's how we all felt.

I actually went into the army in Gisborne. Because I'd been working away from town when my fiancé was killed I went back home. And the next day somebody I knew at the Drill Hall rang to say, 'We hear you're back in town. What about coming down and helping with the medical boards?'

So with dark glasses and swollen eyes I went down there and I'd been typing away on these medical boards for three days when one of the men put a piece of paper in front of me and said, 'You've got to sign this, you're in the army now.'

'Am I really?' I said. 'I don't know whether I want to be!'

So I was in the army there for two years before I went overseas. And I'll tell you this, that a lot of those men who went away from Gisborne—you know they're all sworn in on a Bible?—well, a lot of them were sworn in on my Collins

Neva before going overseas, 1942

dictionary. Because the Area Officer could not find his Bible sometimes, he used to rush through the door and say, 'Get me your dictionary, quickly!' And he'd put his thumb along the spine and cover the word 'dictionary'. 'I don't think it'll make any difference,' he'd say.

It never entered my head to go overseas, but then when army headquarters decided to send clerical girls, I said, 'Oh boy, yes that'd be great.' Full of adventure. But you see— sending clerical girls overseas was a very important decision. They knew there'd be a lot of animosity amongst the men because we would be the *only* ones who were taking jobs from the men. Girls in the clubs and hospitals weren't taking their jobs but we were.

So only 16 of us were sent to begin with, and we had to be very vetted, because of this criticism that would be forthcoming. They told us that we were 'specially chosen'. We all had to go to Wellington and sit tests and so forth, so we could not be criticised on that count.

And we finally got away to Italy. There was animosity for about a week, till the men thought, 'Oh, it's not bad having these girls around.' But you see, we were taking their jobs, and they just thought we were all over there for a jolly good time, but we worked extremely hard.

Every girl was a top-flight secretary and dedicated to her work, and they did have a good time too. Plenty of parties. Yes, I suppose some of them went with the thought that they were going to have a good time. But I don't think when we left

WAAC Clerical Division, Mirimar Camp, 1944. Neva is fourth from right in the front row

New Zealand some of the girls realised that that 'good time' was going to have these tragic little bits on the side.
We were at one stage only eight miles behind the front line. Fellows would come down and have dinner with us or there would be a party, and the next day they were back and oh— killed . . . You see?
This happened with a particular person that I knew, who came with another fellow and had a meal with us and next day had his head blown off. He was in a tank and it was bombed and one man jumped that way and Brian jumped this way. The other man had not a scratch on him and Brian's head was knocked off.

So you see your sense of having a good time was certainly levelled out, and you lived with that every day, of course. There was no alternative but to live with it. You just went on working. You had some very subdued moments, of course.

Did you feel that you were secondary to men?

No, I never felt that. I just felt I was me, doing a job. I never felt secondary. Do you think I should have? No, I don't think any of us did feel like that . . . I mean we weren't going to be killed in action, but we went there to do our job. And we did it very well.

I was first placed in the Military Secretary's office and he was called 'God', because his job was to promote and demote officers and give out all the citations. Another girl and I were put in his office, and we were called 'the angels in God's office'!

I was later sent across the road in charge of distributing the ciphers that arrived. A lot were secret of course. Some were called 'TOP SECRET' and were on different coloured papers. I had this wonderful experience one day when a fellow from Ciphers brought in some messages—I was a fresh-air fiend and my french doors were open onto a balcony. Just as the officer came in there was a *phoo* of wind and a top secret message flew out the window behind me. So we hung out the window and we watched it settle on an Italian casa roof.

We laughed and laughed, and then this fellow said to me, 'I know, I know, I've got to go and get the bloody thing.' So he tore downstairs and got a ladder from somewhere and retrieved this Top Secret message! Never told anybody—we kept that to ourselves.

When army headquarters in Wellington found this experiment worked so well, they sent another 100 Clerical Division girls over, and the girl who was in charge of us was sent back to Egypt.

By this time we were at Senigallia, midway up Italy. Somebody had to be commissioned and put in charge when she left, and I was the one, which absolutely amazed me because I was one of the youngest.

Suddenly from being just one of the girls and being very lively, I was in charge of the group, responsible! I was much more slack with them discipline-wise, because I thought they

NZ Army Administration headquarters, Senigallia, Italy, 1945. Neva is third from right, second row

NZ Army secretaries, wearing leather jerkins to keep out the cold, Senigallia, Italy, 1945. Neva is fifth from the left

can't possibly do anything that I haven't already done myself.
And I'm not going to stay up until one o'clock in the morning
if I've gone round beds and found 'she's not home'. I'll just go
to bed and ask her about it in the morning.

    We had one strange little episode . . . one of the guards
came calling me—I was in bed sound asleep—'Come down.
Quick! Two of the guards across the road are having a fight!'
I tore down in my nightie and bare feet across to where these
people were.
A little Italian admirer of mine, who wrote a little letter each
day with a red rose and gave it to the guards to give to me . . .
he was there too. The two guards were punching each other
up, and this little Fabio was in the way and got a black eye.
I said, 'I don't think this is the place for me in my nightdress
. . . I'm going to bed. If you want to kill each other—kill
each other.'
Well, they were both alive in the morning and I don't know
what happened. A lot of those problems solved themselves.

    We had two girls we had to send home with what they call
'anxiety neurosis'. One of them went into an asylum.
In both cases it was male relationships and the total
emotional confusion. It was obviously sexual pressure.
The girl from Wellington was just so beautiful, and so aware of
her beauty . . . every night she used to wear sticking plaster
here and there on her face so she wouldn't get wrinkles. She
had a proper sort of league of nations of admirers, and I think
she—it was too much for her. She had this wonderful ability to

look quite different from the rest of us in our uniforms because somebody would give her, for instance, a white duffle coat, which she had no hesitation in wearing when you weren't allowed to, and she looked as if she was out of *Vogue* magazine. She had all these wonderful romances, and that really confused her I think.

And then the other girl—she was away with the fairies . . . we had to send her to hospital. And when she was there, she got out of bed—she had a little teddy bear—and ran along the beach naked clutching the teddy bear.

So we sent her to a British psychiatric centre and I went up to see her, and she was quite deranged, so we had to send her home . . . she was young and rather sheltered and very Catholic and that could also have contributed to her breakdown. I think she was totally torn emotionally.

The emotional strain was very strong on us girls, extremely strong.

I don't think some knew what they were getting into and a few absolutely could not cope with these situations.

A lot of the emotion came from the men and their attention to us because there were so many men, and so few girls.

And those men—naturally they hadn't seen a girl for a long time, especially a girl from New Zealand, and they wanted to talk.

Most of them were very happy just to talk. I'm a good listener and I allowed them to get rid of all their thoughts and stuff. They loved to talk about home, wives, fiancées. And some

NZ Army personnel in front of St. Peters, Rome. Neva is seventh from left

would say, 'Oh I wish my wife could meet you. She would be so glad that I know you over here.' And I thought, oh dear, I wouldn't be too sure about that—I'd been at home with a fiancé overseas, and I wouldn't like to hear, 'I've met this lovely girl, and she and I have wonderful times together.' Might be perfectly innocent, but you wouldn't want to know about it. So I always hoped these guys did not write that sort of thing home.

    But you did play quite an important role in their lives because they were in a totally abnormal situation. Totally *abnormal*. Suddenly, here was somebody they could speak to about *ordinary* things. And they would talk about how they felt about being in the front line, and how they felt when one of their buddies was killed, and how much they *longed* for the war to be over, and it all seemed hopeless . . . this was one of the things that came out over and over again.
The futility.
I was very angry a lot of the time at the total futility of what I was in amongst. Total futility. You'd meet someone, an air force guy perhaps, and he'd go back to his unit and you'd think oh . . . another sortie going over—I hope he comes back. And they sometimes did and sometimes didn't.
That emotional thing was a huge part of our existence.

Did people fall in love very easily?

Yes. In and out.

And it presented problems because some of the men just . . . they fell in love with you immediately. Just because you were there. That was really what it was about, and if you listened to them, then that was extra special. They *really* fell for you. They believed themselves to be in love with you. And some of them took it for granted that, because that's how they felt, necessarily you felt the same way about them. And you didn't. That was another tricky little emotional problem to deal with because you wouldn't for all the world make them unhappy. You had to explain, 'Look, we are in very abnormal times, and we shouldn't even be thinking about these things. Let's wait until we go home, then we'll know where we're at.'
Some of them took that nicely and some were furious.
And they were *all* so lovely. A lot of them wrote you lovely letters and lovely poems. Some of them not good poems, but thoughtful . . . how they felt about you. They often sent photographs of themselves which sometimes we used to laugh about because we never asked them to . . . 'How conceited, what did you send that for,' . . . you know? We had these little jokes sometimes.

Under these strange circumstances you were saying goodbye with the prospect of never saying hello again. Weren't you tempted to get physically involved with these men?

Physically it was very tempting. I mean, you had these wonderful men kissing you goodnight, and you were female

and he was male. It was awfully tempting to go overboard physically. But I didn't. I didn't at all.
Very tempted. Oh yes. It was very hard not to sometimes. Mind you, circumstances were against you because there was nowhere much to indulge in sex. I mean if you're really keen I suppose you'd find somewhere . . . in a muddy tomato patch or something, not much fun, but no . . . it was too confusing with too many guys, you see. There were too many of them, you could never say, 'He's the one for me.' Because the next one was just as lovely, and the next one again.
I had some wonderful male friends. Some of them still pay me attention all these years later. Come and see me, and ring me up.
But, you know, it was all very real, but very confusing, so I didn't want to let myself go physically with them because I had myself to answer to.

I rather reluctantly became engaged amid all this confusion. I wasn't entirely sure that I liked him more than I liked the others, and I didn't love him the way I loved Geoff. Because I never have.
He was a Cameron Highlander I met in Rome when we were on leave. There was a group of us and the fellow who was my escort returned to his unit and this Jock Schofield said, 'I'll take Neva over.'
And we had a lovely time in Rome. Then he kept coming down from wherever he was to us, and he was very popular

Jock Schofield, a Queen's Own Cameron Highlander. Neva's fiancé, this photograph was taken shortly before he died, 20 April 1945, aged 25

because he brought us cases of apples, and all sorts of things. And—*and* New Zealand butter, which they had in their English mess, where we had margarine in our New Zealand mess.

So we had some lovely times and I did get engaged to him three weeks before the end of the war. Just before he went off to Belgium.

He was killed, almost immediately, on my birthday.

So when peace was declared, I had to sit in the Garrison Theatre at the Thanksgiving Service representing New Zealand women, up on the stage, with the padre, with the brigadier. And, looking at that big theatre full of soldiers thanking God the war was over, I tell you I didn't hear one word. I had to steel myself not to listen, or I'd have cried and made an idiot of myself. I had to just gaze out into the audience. I had to look at how the men in the front row were sitting—were their feet crossed or not—and count the heads, and do anything to fill in time until it was over.

And when it was over, one man—he knew what had happened to me—came and collected me. And we sat on our marble steps and he held me in his arms because he knew how I felt. He was a cipher—sergeant major—he was married when he went overseas and his wife was pregnant. And one night when he was on duty a message came through. 'Tell Sergeant Major Moodie that his wife died in childbirth.' And he was the one that took the message.

So he knew—he understood how I felt then.

    We had 18 days' English leave towards the end of the war,

and I went and visited Jock's people, never having met them. And I slept in Jock's bedroom. I put my beret in the drawer with his officer's cap. His trunk had just come back from Belgium, and it was under the window like a coffin. I slept in his bed. And went to a memorial service at his old school a couple of days later. It was a terrible experience.

You couldn't escape being emotionally or mentally affected by the war, but were you ever in any physical danger?

Something unforgettable happened when we were in Santa Spirito where the only thing to do in the evenings, in the lovely long Italian twilights, was to walk around the waterfront.
A little fishing village it was. Some of us had been to a dance at a Royal Air Force camp one night. We used to go to these dances incidentally, in the back of a five-ton truck, sitting on chairs with air force jackets around us if it was cold.
Anyway, deputed to look after me at this particular dance was a little fellow called Mac whose name I can't remember now. He came to the mess with some of the others for a meal later, and he and I walked around the waterfront.
The village was very tiny. We went past the houses to a line of flat rocks—and we walked over the rocks to the water's edge and we sat and we talked.

After a little while Mac said, 'I think we'd better go. Behind us there are three strange-looking men.'

Neva outside the Nissan hut, where Neva shared a room, Santa Spirito, 1944

I looked around and the men were on the road, which was say, 100 yards away, one soldier, one soldier, one soldier . . . we thought other than swimming home, we had to get back on that road.
So back we went, and these three closed in.
One of them had a knife which he put to Mac's chest, and in very broken English—they were Palestinian Arabs in army uniform—put this knife to Mac's chest and told him they would all have sex with me and then Mac could have sex with me.
At that Mac, who was quite a short fellow, punched this man in the face. And I thought, 'Oh, Mac will be dead.'
At the same moment one of the others picked me up and threw me over a shoulder and took off into a ploughed field with me. Running, running, running. I yelled. 'Help, English, help!'
A second soldier put his hand over my mouth as they ran on—quite a long way, and I was thrown on the ground.
I was sure Mac was dead on the road. They stripped my clothes off me. And the one with the knife knelt at my head—he had the knife there on my forehead—and one was holding my legs. The third had taken off his trousers, and here he was with this great big penis and here was I wearing nothing but a sanitary towel—the big bulky sanitary towel that we all had and . . . I wasn't frightened. This is amazing to me now in retrospect. I don't know how I got through that physically or mentally.
I was so angry, and I thought—I thought I was fighting for my

life, and I think I was. I fought, I kicked, I wriggled, I squirmed and it felt like hours, but in fact it was 20 minutes. Which is a long time to be in that situation; but then I saw a row of torchlights come over a stone wall and I called out, 'Here!' And at that, the three Palestinian Arabs got up and ran away, and then one came back—he might have dropped his knife I thought—I held onto his ankle, but my hands are pretty small, and he got away.

    The soldiers with the torches ran after those people. Mac arrived by my side. 'I'll go with them,' he said. And I said, 'Please don't, *please* don't!'
I was standing up, and I didn't care if he was the entire Royal Air Force. There was I wearing a sanitary towel. I groped around on the ground and found my clothes and I got dressed.

    There was a British unit just along the road and this is where Mac had run to and where we then went. It was a unit to which these Palestinian Arabs happened to be attached. Mac was terribly upset because he felt that what had happened was his fault, he was supposed to be protecting me.

    So they took me home to our mess, where I was sharing a room with a girl from Napier. She was sound asleep and I woke her up and told her everything and then I went to bed and I stayed awake all night.
In the morning, two officers from the British unit came to our headquarters, alerted the colonel from A Branch who was in charge of all of us, and round to our mess they came. Breakfast time.

And I was towelled up for not reporting this the night before.
I hadn't dreamt of reporting it the night before. You know—I
didn't report it—I just went to bed. Stupid in retrospect.
Anyway, it was duly reported and our provosts, our policemen,
had a fellow called Sid take a long statement from me. I typed
what he was telling me to type—he was asking me the
questions then I had to type my answers to him and I can
remember him asking a particular question.
'Oh for God's sake,' I said, 'stop talking as if we're married.'
He was very angry with me because he thought I should have
reported to him the night before.

    Then there was an identification parade which was
absolutely ghastly. Ghastly. Because all these Palestinian Arabs
looked totally evil.
I recognised one, Akad.

    We had a summary of evidence, in a town further north.
Headquarters let another girl travel with me.
And it was very hard to find this town, Arrezzo, because the
retreating Germans had turned all the signs in the wrong
directions, so we got lost several times.
The summary of evidence was pretty awful, and it was all
done by the English unit. They handled this. New Zealanders
did not. In charge was a Major Carl Parker who wore a purple
and white polka dot cravat, with a purple and white polka dot
hanky in his pocket.
We were in a hotel—it had been bombed and there was no
glass in the windows, and no water supply so each room had a

bucket of water. I didn't have one in my room as I was supposed to have, so I walked along the passages—saw a door open, saw a bucket of water—went in and took it. Then the little manager of the hotel, Ray someone, came up and said, 'Major Parker wants to see you down in the office about tomorrow.' So I went down, and this Major Carl Parker said to the manager, 'Oh, by the way, some cad's pinched my water! Could you get me another bucketful?'—it was the boss's water that I'd stolen.

Later on we had the court martial itself. And that was even worse—I can't remember now who was there, but the accused of course, myself and Mac who was terrified, interpreters, a defence fellow, and Major Carl Parker.

There were things I could not say. I could not say the word f-u-c-k, I still find it hard. And I wouldn't say it. Of course it was very necessary, so I was given a piece of foolscap paper—'Please print it in capital letters' was the order, which I did, and the paper was handed back.
The word was announced in a very loud voice, and all these men, except Mac, sniggered.
I thought, 'You awful people. How can you snigger?'

Akad got five years' hard labour. I was told by the English officer in charge of the unit that before coming to Italy, that same man had been up on a murder charge in Egypt, and it hadn't been proved. So he was really bad.
His unit wrote to warn me about reprisals afterwards. It never happened, because the war was going north so quickly.

We moved and that unit moved, and we all got thrown in different directions.
So nothing else happened as far as that was concerned. It was a shattering experience, and in a way it didn't put me off men, but it put me off—in my two marriages—it put me off men who only think of you as a sex object, which both my husbands did after a little while.
So it affected my life terribly.
    During the trial I was made to feel that I was 'looking for it' . . .
'Why were you there in that isolated place?' You know?
As if you wanted to have sex on a lumpy old rock surface, and that's not what I was there for.
But you are made to feel dirty, a prostitute, all those things, and when I hear girls say this, I know what they're talking about. And when people say laughingly, 'If you're raped you might as well lie back and enjoy it' I have to leave the room. I can't say, 'Shut up, you don't know what you're talking about.' I just quietly go away.
Because they think they're being funny.

I'm amazed now, after all this time, to re-read in my diary—
I kept four very full volumes and typed it all back when I came home—
and I was amazed to re-read a lot of it, and find out how often I was very very angry. This was not mentioned outwardly only in my diary.

Would you like me to read just one little bit?

'10th of April 1945. Our boys in boots and all now. The volume of stuff going up is terrific. Last night there were sounds like shelling or bombing quite close to here. And the villas shook as though it was a quake. Most of the girls failed to sleep, and though for a short while I wondered what use our guard would be if any of the enemy did appear on the scene, and how much some of the girls would panic. I was very sleepy, and I went to bed. Trains are rattling up all day and night with supplies, and the air is constantly a whirr of planes on their way to cause destruction. I stood on the balcony and watched wave upon wave go over and thought of Geoff, and lovely Peter Fay who is up with Number Three Squadron, imagined him with one of their flights, and wondered if he'd come back. Became so infuriated deep down inside—so absolutely bloody silly that these chaps should give their young lives. Felt perturbed for the rest of the day.'

At the end of the war I stayed behind in Italy with the rear party.
I didn't want to come home. I was still too emotionally upset over Jock, you see, and I didn't want to come home in that frame of mind.
So I stayed behind. And I actually almost went to Japan. A few of us wanted to and we were going, but as we almost had a foot on the ship, the brigadier in charge said, 'Take it off. None of you are going.'

I wasn't ready to come home, emotionally, but I had to, and that was that.

Coming home like that was terribly confusing . . . very exciting to see the land of course.
Although I was still rebelling against arriving at all, I had that terrific affection for the country, but I was well . . . not very glad about being here at that particular moment.
And apart from that, I'd outgrown Gisborne, I think. Most of my friends, young friends, had moved away,
so I felt a bit of a foreigner there.

Somebody rang when I wasn't home, to say that they would like me to give a talk at the something or other—the Country Women's Institute, or the Embroidery Club perhaps, and Mum said . . . 'Oh, Neva's far too shy to do that.'
I don't think my mother knew me very well at that time, but she spoke on my behalf because *she* was shy.
Well, I didn't want to be in that environment. Not my scene. Gisborne people had this extraordinary idea that we'd just had a wonderful time. And I remember one of our neighbours saying to me, 'Oh well, now you've had all that wonderful experience, I suppose you'll settle down and get married.' And I just wanted to kill her.
They really thought that's what we would want to do, and we weren't ready for that. They had no idea what that experience had done to us.
I was amazed at how many of my girls did not marry.
They were all so attractive and so talented. I would say half of

them did not marry. It always amazes me. All got very good jobs afterwards—became quite important in their line but . . . I suppose there was a dearth of men, there had to be, didn't there?

Whose photograph did you keep in your wallet?

Geoff's.

All through the war?

Even when I was engaged to Jock.

Did he know?

Oh, no . . . many secrets. I don't think we meant them to be secrets. But they come out as that now . . . only because they hadn't been revealed.

Neva Clarke McKenna was awarded an MID (Mentioned In Despatches for Distinguished Service) during the war.

Return of soldiers on furlough. War Effort Collection, ATL

Appendix I: Chronology of women's work 1940-1946*

1940
Feb — Appeals made for more female labour for factories
Mar — Women into wartime work—sewing battledress
Jun — Suspension of labour legislation allows women to work night-shifts if satisfactory conveyance home arranged
Jul — Manpower regulations establish national register of all persons over 16 to be directed into industry and other work

1941
Apr — First ten women police begin training
Aug — Many jobs in Public Service taken over by women: 1,400 increase in two years
Oct — Increasing numbers of women in traditional male jobs in industry

1942
Mar — Women 20-21 years required to register for work—widows of servicemen and caring for children aged under 16 years exempt
May — Women as hotel porters and railway station porters
Aug — All women 20-23 required to register for work
Sep — Women 24-30 called upon to register for work
Oct — Women's minimum weekly pay set—£2.17.6 (£5.0.0. for men)
Nov — Maori women liable for registration under Manpower regulations
Dec — By end of 1942 approximately 224,000 women in civilian employment (1939—180,000)

1943
Jan — 10,000 women in government departments
Feb — Women aged 18-19 required to register for work
May — Women's part-time work in factories increases
Jul — In Wellington, about 140 women as tram conductors—on equal pay with men. 150 women as herd testers
Sep — Manufacturers protest against women in services because of industry labour shortages (1944—7,837 women in armed forces, including 838 overseas)
Dec — Women university and training college students work as hospital ward maids and kitchen hands

1944
Jan — Women up to 40 years of age required to register for essential work
Mar — 75,000 women in essential industries—153,000 in other employment
Public Service Women's committee formed to fight for equal pay and opportunity

1945
Mar — Renewed campaign for women workers for industry and hospitals. 157,508 women registered for employment for essential industries
Jun — Women 40 years of age and over, wives and widows of servicemen given leave from manpower controls

Dec   First women appointed as welfare officers in Maori Affairs Department

1946

Mar   Factories Act passed—continuation of provisions restricting women workers from night shifts and overtime and from metal working and cleaning machinery, except over summer when women's labour needed in canning and jam factories

* Excludes voluntary work or those in the services.
Compiled from the chronology of events in *Women in Wartime*, pp 264–275.

Appendix II: *Women in World War II (1939–1945)*
                        Oral History Project: 1991–1994

The project was commissioned by Gaylene Preston Productions. Stage I was funded by the New Zealand Lottery Grants Board. Stage II was funded by the 1993 Women's Suffrage Trust Whakatu Wahine. Support for all stages of the project was given by the Alexander Turnbull Library.

Objectives
- To record the hitherto undocumented oral testimonies of a group of women who were aged between 20 and 40 and living in New Zealand during the period of the Second World War.
- To create an oral record, to supplement the official Government war records and other records of the Second World War, for archival purposes, and to provide a resource for a proposed documentary feature film and a book.
- The project was devised to be carried out in three stages.

Background
Surprisingly little has been documented about the war from the women's perspective and existing records tell little about the everyday role of women during the war years. The focus of this project is the women's memories and perceptions of the war as well as the examination of the short-term and long-term impact of this historical event on their individual lives. (While the primary objective was to generate an archival resource, it was also regarded as an opportunity to provide training. Some of the work was carried out by new/less experienced oral history researchers under supervision.)

Research
Resources included:
- The Oral History Centre and World War II collection, the Alexander Turnbull Library, National Library of New Zealand.
- *Women in Wartime: New Zealand Women Tell Their Story*, by Lauris Edmond with Carolyn Milward, Government Printing Office, Wellington, New Zealand, 1986.
- *The Home Front*, Vols 1 and 2, Nancy Taylor, Historical Publications Branch, Department of Internal Affairs, 1986.
- Personal documents and recollections of a diverse group of women who contacted Gaylene Preston Productions after project publicity.
- New Zealand Oral History Archive's chronology of national and international events.
- The World War II film collection, National Archives of New Zealand.
- A survey of visual documentation carried out by Alison Parr and commissioned by Gaylene Preston Productions.

Interviewees
For Stage I, 20 interviewees were selected on a random rather than predetermined basis, on the grounds that every woman has her own story and unique experiences.

Unlike Stage I, the selection for Stages II and III was more directive to ensure that gaps were filled, that the services were more proportionally represented and to follow themes which resulted from the analysis of Stage I.

To some extent the interviewees were chosen as individuals first—their wartime experiences came second. The base criterion was that each interviewee was aged between 20 and 40 in 1939 (in the latter stages, six women who were schoolgirls during wartime were included).

Endeavours were made to get a mixed group in terms of socio-economic background and wartime experience (about ten percent of New Zealand women of eligible age enlisted in wartime military services) and effort was made to ensure that a demographically representative number of Maori women were recorded. (There were also geographical constraints imposed by the budget.)

The 66 interviewees were chosen from a wide range of women who personally contacted the project, names submitted by service organisations and interested individuals, and women identified by the interviewers and others involved in the project.

Statistics

Age: Most of the 66 interviewees were in their seventies at the time of the interview. The eldest was 85 and the youngest 59.

Ethnicity: 16 Maori, three Chinese, three German/Jewish, 44 Pakeha New Zealanders.

Wartime service: Eight were in Wartime Womens' Military Services (WAAC, WAAF, WRNZNS); seven served overseas during the Second World War (hospital ships, General Hospital Middle East/North Africa/Italy, QAIMNS (Queen Alexandra Imperial Military Hospital), naval mines division at Rabaul, clerical, commissioned officer NZ Army Headquarters Administration); 12 were manpowered during the war (three in EPS).

Several enlisted as VADs or did voluntary service with the Red Cross and the St John's Ambulance. A significant number were actively involved in entertainment/concert parties during the war.

Wartime employment: 13 interviewees were not in any form of paid employment during the Second World War—six were school students, the others described themselves as housewives. The majority of interviewees were involved in some form of voluntary wartime work.

Occupations included: tram conductress, telephonist, farmer, farmworker, nurse, nursery and kindergarten employee, cook, clerical assistant, florist, public servant, shorthand typist, War Office typist, office clerk, clerical assistant, secretary, shop assistant, waitress, journalist, school dental nurse, domestic, factory worker, transport/delivery operator.

Marital status/family: 31 interviewees were married before or during the war. 35 (including six schoolgirls) were single. Not all the women married post-war; at least three remained single. A small number of the women were divorced. A larger number had married twice. The majority were widowed at the time of the interview (13 out of 20 in Stage II).

Several had husbands who served overseas during the war—two husbands were POWs. Two women were married to conscientious objectors who were imprisoned during the war. Six were war widows.

Collectively they had 45 children born before or during the war.

There were three lots of sisters, three lots of sisters-in-law, and four were connected through marriage.

The Interviews
Interviewers: The interviewers were: Julie Benjamin, Jenny Bush, Cathy Casey, Sarah Dalton, Michelle Erai, Susan Fowke, Judith Fyfe, Alison Parr, Queenie Rikihana-Hyland, Brita McVeigh, Jane Tolerton and Johanna Woods.

The interviewer's task was to gather personal histories of the women's psychological and emotional development during the war. Briefing for interviewers emphasised the importance of gathering domestic detail (in both a practical and emotional sense) because how events affected and changed individuals is as interesting as the events themselves.

Interviews: The interviews had a basic structure in order to allow for comparisons and to give context and control, but allowed flexibility and the possibility of pursuing areas of special interest and knowledge. Standard life history and topic-related oral history methods were used. The interviews were divided into three main areas:
- life pre-war (biographies, childhood, personal chronology)
- life during the war (personal experiences and observations)
- life post-war (up till the present).

The interviews were recorded in the interviewees' own homes during the period 1991 to 1994. The duration of each interview ranged from one to five hours—the majority were three hours. The project has generated approximately 180 hours of taped interviews.

Accompanying the tapes are folders which include a time-coded summary of the interview, career details, genealogical information, a technical report and photographs.

The Abstract
This is a guide to the contents of the tape. It is a written time-coded summary of the contents with proper names, places and subjects highlighted.

Abstracters: The abstracters were: Jannette Day, Judith Fyfe, Susan Fowke, Jean Harton, Megan Hutching, Sarah Lambie and Johanna Woods.

The task of the abstracter is, as faithfully as possible, to supply an accurate written précis of the information given by the interviewee—a fair summary of what the researcher can hear on the tape itself.

Tairongo Amoamo compiled the summarised translation of the bilingual tapes.

Access to Collection
Tapes, photographs and other material related to the project are in the custody of the Alexander Turnbull Library, National

Library of New Zealand, Wellington. The collection is accessible there, through the Oral History Centre, for research purposes in accordance with the stipulation of the individual's agreement documents.

A written *agreement* was signed at the conclusion of the interview allowing unrestricted or restricted use of the material. This agreement is between the interviewee, Gaylene Preston Productions and the Alexander Turnbull Library.

The agreements are strictly followed in order to keep faith with the interviewees who have provided frank and often sensitive information.

Copyright in the tape recordings and accompanying material generated by this project is held by Gaylene Preston Productions.

(Eight edited interviews, accompanied by Gil Hanly portraits, are currently part of the long-term *Voices* exhibition at the Museum of New Zealand/Te Papa Tongarewa.)

Conclusion

This project is a collection of the personal views, experiences and memories of the Second World War by 66 New Zealand women. No attempt has been made to correct or interpret the information. The taped material is in a raw unedited state. Gaylene Preston Productions has endeavoured to carry out the research and interviews with objectivity and in accordance with the National Oral History Association of New Zealand (NOHANZ) Code of Ethical Practice.

The project is also a valuable record of styles of speech and use of language which are constantly changing in New Zealand. Several of the interviews are recorded in both Maori and English. English was the second language for a number of the interviewees.

The themes and issues that surfaced in the material recorded in Stage I, were probed and pursued further in Stages II and III. In particular more attention was given to the period of readjustment post-war: the long-term effect that war had on the mental and physical health of the men who served overseas and the subsequent impact on the lives of the women and the children.

The Women in World War II Oral History Project answers such questions as 'was the war the best, the worst, the least or the most interesting, a liberating or insignificant time of your life?' The diversity of experience and reaction was significant—for some women it was a time of heightened social life and emotions whilst for others the management of homes and families carried on from day to day regardless of a major historical event.

It is too late to talk to their mothers—that generation of women who having recovered from the loss of their brothers and fathers in the First World War then went through the trauma again as wives and mothers in the Second World War. We can only regret that lost opportunity. There is an urgent need to ask more women, 'What happened to you during the war?' This generation of New Zealand women now in their seventies and eighties is rapidly diminishing. Very soon we will be left with only the memory of the memory.

Gaylene Preston Productions wishes to acknowledge those whose enthusiastic assistance made this important project possible. In particular, project co-ordinator and project managers, the directors and staff of the Oral History Centre, Alexander Turnbull Library, the New Zealand Lottery Grants Board, and the 1993 Women's Suffrage Trust Whakatu Wahine, and of course the interviewees for their co-operation and contribution to a valuable resource for future researchers.